THE ONE & DONE
COOKBOOK

87+ Plant-Based
DINNERS FOR EASY
Weeknight COOKING

By BETSY FREEMAN

STONE PIER
PRESS

Stone Pier Press
San Francisco, California

ISBN: 9781734901160

Library of Congress Control Number: 2022945762

Names: Freeman, Betsy, author and illustrator. Ellis, Clare, editor.
Title: The One & Done Cookbook: 87+ plant-based dinners for easy
weeknight cooking

Printed in the United States of America

25 24 23 22   1 2 3 4 5 6 7 8

Cover design/illustration by Betsy Freeman
Designed and set in type by Abrah Griggs
Indexing by Elise Hess

TABLE of CONTENTS

STIR FRIES

ONE RECIPE, THREE WAYS

LET'S BEGIN

I'm an avid reader of cookbooks, a relentless seeker of interesting flavor combinations, and a life-long appreciator of vegetables. I appreciate the transformative power of cooking and the way it can turn chopped vegetables dressed with little more than olive oil, salt, and pepper into an altered state of deliciousness.

I manage to have a good time every time I forage for ingredients in my pantry and fridge, pull out a bowl chopping board, and fire up my oven. I love the tactile and sensory rewards of putting together a meal — the peeling, chopping, and grating. The chance to inhale all that freshness. The taste testing.

For me, cooking is a creative outlet that also makes it easier to eat in a way that's healthy and affordable. But I recognize not everyone likes to cook, and a couple of years ago I started asking people why. The reply given most frequently: lack of time. Given that we tend to have time to do the things we enjoy, it's an easy bet that lack of interest is also involved.

As a product designer, I'm used to thinking about more seamless ways for people to interact with the world around them. So I decided to apply that same thinking to cooking to see if I could make it more appealing for people too busy to cook.

Common time sinks include recipes that call for too many ingredients, too many unfamiliar cooking techniques, and too many dishes. I'm familiar with all of these hurdles. I used to cope by regularly serving Trader Joe's ready-made dinners on top of salad greens or brown rice. And what's wrong with that? If you're not wild about cooking, why *not* just heat up pre-made curries, fried rice dishes, or other packaged food?

Here's what helped convince me to switch to home cooking: Cooking up whole ingredients instead of packaged dinners, which are often processed and high in sodium, is just better for you, plus it tends to be less expensive. My experience as an occasional cook had also taught me how much I was missing — the hands-on, near-sensual nature of cooking not to mention the way fresh flavors taste.

1

Once I'd decided to see if I could make healthy cooking easier, I started experimenting with popular recipes. I deliberately skipped steps or consolidated them, left out or swapped in different ingredients, and streamlined the instructions and number of cooking tools to what was most essential. I learned what did and did not work and iterated from there. Design. Test. Refine. Repeat.

Eventually, I learned that cooking need not result in a mountain of dishes in the sink. That one recipe can be served many different ways. And that a single dish can amount to a full dinner, no sides necessary. Mostly I learned that healthy cooking doesn't have to be hard.

Toward that end, I've kept the prepping instructions straightforward and brief. I suggest when to buy an ingredient rather than make it from scratch — canned chickpeas, frozen green beans, and peeled butternut squash can save time and still offer the nutrients and taste you want. Finally, I've kept the cooking fairly simple. Rarely does a dish call for a special technique, and when it does, I break it down for you.

Unlike most cookbooks, these recipes are illustrated — by me. Choosing illustrations over photography is in line with the ethos of the book. This is not aspirational cooking; it's practical, flexible, and whatever you want it to be. While I suggest serving suggestions and toppings, they are only *suggestions*. I leave it to you to decide how you want your dinner to look, and to taste.

How to use this book

Once you're comfortable with the recipes in this book, you may not need to refer to them anymore. They're meant to inspire you to expand upon, and enjoy, your own cooking.

Cooking hacks. In this section (p.5), I share a few of the shortcuts that have helped me enjoy cooking more — like peeled garlic, hand-held blenders, and frozen corn. You might be surprised by the pleasure you get out of cooking when you no longer have to peel the thin skin off garlic in order to mince it — or whatever other task puts you off. Find your pain points and add your own shortcuts to the list.

Built-in flexibility. The recipes are designed to make it easy for you to prepare them. You'll find serving *suggestions* and *optional* ingredients and ingredient *swaps*. They're there to help you use what you already have on hand, get in touch with your preferences, and explore other tastes and textures. I'd love to save you a run to the grocery store, help you make your own calls on what's optional, and maybe ignite an interest in some new seasoning or protein options.

Sauces. Adding sauce or dressing to a dish can tie together the ingredients and enhance the flavors. I like sauces so much I've dedicated a section of this book to them (p.145). But in the spirit of one-and-done simplicity, I've left the choice of using them to you. Every one of the sauces can be replaced with a store bought version or eliminated entirely. I just want to give you the option.

Cooked grains. The grain bowl is a foundational element of the one-and-done regimen because it's healthy, and easy to assemble and customize. This means you'll find that many recipes ask for "cooked grains." It's one of those ingredients you can just buy — precooked rice, quinoa, and polenta are easily available as is frozen cauliflower rice. But not all grains are easy to find pre-cooked — take farro, for instance.

When cooking grains, the best advice is to follow package directions because they vary, from one rice to another, for instance. I also recommend cooking in batches to use throughout the week. To add richness, measure out a tablespoon or so of olive oil while cooking. For more flavor, stir in some fresh herbs, such as parsley, thyme or basil. To bring out the best in your grain, add a pinch of salt while cooking, and another sprinkle at the end.

Prep to table time. Each recipe includes an estimate of how much time it takes to chop, measure, cook, and otherwise prepare a meal — it's just easier to plan dinner that way. Because you're the one choosing to cook grains, or take advantage of the pre-cooked option, grain prep is not part of the calculation.

Plant-based. This cookbook is plant-based, which means the recipes are vegetarian with an option to veganize. I use plant-based oils rather than butter, and plant-based milk for dairy milk. I often recommend cheese, especially for toppings, with the understanding that there's a vegan option for almost every one. One of my go-to cheese alternatives is fortified nutritional yeast, which lends a creamy cheesy texture and flavor to dishes, along with lots of vitamin B. I leave out eggs except when it's a critical ingredient, as in quiche. Finally, I have a weakness for plain Greek yogurt as a topping — just putting it out there. Dairy-free sour cream and yogurt exist and the yogurt topping is just a suggestion, but I do love what a dollop of plain Greek yogurt can do for a dish.

Low waste. I've included a brief guide to cutting up vegetables (p. 149). It describes techniques, as in, what does mincing onions look like, along with suggestions for minimizing waste. The leafy green part of a leek, for instance, is often tossed. Keep it! (All but the toughest topmost part.) It's full of vitamin C and it tastes good. Broccoli florets aren't the only part worth eating; so are the stalks, if you slice off the tough outsides before chopping them up, and so on. Throughout the recipes, I list the full can of beans or tomatoes wherever possible and the whole vegetable so you don't have to store (or toss) the leftovers. In cases where I ask for, say, half an onion or two cups of broccolini, I invite you to ignore the instructions and use up the entire vegetable.

Recipe-free. Knowing a few cooking techniques and flavor profiles can free you to make good dinners without resorting to a recipe. In the recipe-free section of this book (p.141), I offer suggestions for assembling a variety of grain bowls. I list examples of vegetables and seasonings that work well together along with proteins, grains, and toppings to choose among. Note: If you want to expand your flavor knowledge base, I recommend borrowing or buying a copy of *The Flavor Bible*, by Andrew Domenburg and Karen Page. It's a guide to which herbs and spices work well with what vegetables, and I consider it indispensable to freestyle cooking.

COOKING HACKS

One reason I find cooking relaxing is because I double down on the fun bits — the chopping, stirring, and experimenting with flavors. How'd I arrive at this happy place in the kitchen? I found ways to cut out the parts I find tedious — like soaking beans and gutting winter squash.

Some steps you don't want to skip — like rinsing canned beans after you've drained them. It's an excellent way to cut the sodium content. But you don't have to peel garlic or even carrots, if you'd rather not. (Though do wash your carrots.)

The following shortcuts help me make more time for the fun stuff, like eating. I welcome you to come up with your own.

Rely on a few pre-prepped ingredients.

Peeled garlic. Many stores now carry peeled cloves. The elite chefs of the world might beg to differ but I haven't been able to detect any difference in taste, plus peeling garlic sometimes makes me want to punch a wall.

Canned vegetable broth. Boiling chopped vegetables until they're soft and then pouring them through a strainer before throwing them away is not how I want to spend a weekend, so I buy my broth. If you want to cut back on packaging, buy packets of vegetable bouillon paste and mix them with some water. Vegetable stock is another option; the difference is that broth is seasoned.

Squeezed lemon juice. Lemon juice is an essential ingredient in many recipes. Some cooks use it almost like salt because it adds a nice, bright flavor. I think fresh lemon juice is best but bottled lemon juice will do in a pinch.

Peeled and chopped winter squash. Though I love the farm-to-table idea of picking out my own butternut squash, it can be a grind to cook, peel, and gut. So I tend to go

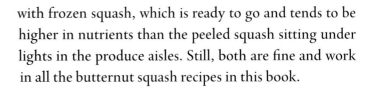

with frozen squash, which is ready to go and tends to be higher in nutrients than the peeled squash sitting under lights in the produce aisles. Still, both are fine and work in all the butternut squash recipes in this book.

Pre-cooked rice, polenta, or quinoa. Though I usually cook my grains, I always have a few pre-cooked options on hand in case I'm strapped for time. I also appreciate that it means one fewer pot to clean up.

Measuring pasta. It's easy to cook pasta — just follow the instructions on the package. But measuring how many ounces to cook to get three cups, for instance, can be trickier. I've used ounces to be consistent with package directions. But the following rule of thumb can be useful for turning ounces into cups — both uncooked and cooked.

Long pasta (spaghetti, linguini, fettucini, angel hair): 2 ounces of long pasta, or about ½ cup uncooked, is equal to 1 cup of cooked pasta. To measure 2 ounces, hold enough dry pasta in your hand to equal the diameter of a quarter.

Short pasta (orecchiette, farfalle or bow tie, fusilli, penne, elbow macaroni, medium shells): Generally, 2 ounces of dry pasta, or about ½ cup, yields 1 to 1¼ cups of cooked pasta.

Frozen vegetables. Fresh gets all the good press, but frozen food is nutrient-dense because it is picked and packed at the peak of ripeness. Frozen vegetables can be roasted and sautéed, and also do beautifully in soups, stews, and mashes. Another big plus: They come husked, trimmed, and peeled. In general, you can use fresh, frozen, and canned vegetables interchangeably in a recipe.

Canned beans. Relying on cooked beans was a game-changer for one of our testers, who was used to soaking and slow-cooking them. This simple shortcut "drastically" cut the time she spent making dinner. The one thing you shouldn't skip: draining and rinsing the beans. Doing so sharply reduces the sodium content per serving.

Streamline the clean-up process.

Immersion blender. This handy little tool allows you to happily pulverize vegetables without sloshing around hot, steamy liquids and dirtying hard-to-clean standing blenders. Creamy soups? No problem.

Lidded jars. Shake your dressing or sauce in a lidded jar, and skip the bowl and whisk. Whatever you don't use gets capped, and goes right in the fridge. I've found that an old salsa container or jam jar generally does the trick.

Parchment paper. Use parchment paper instead of oil on your sheet pans when roasting vegetables or anything sticky. Nothing except my admiration sticks to it, which makes cleaning up a snap. When you're through, toss it into the compost.

Clean-as-you-go. My intent with this book is to give you recipes that don't rely on extensive ingredient lists, steps, or tools. But cooking is manual so I recommend embracing the slowness of it, and tidying up as you go. While the vegetables are sautéing, wash your cutting board. While the soup is coming to a boil, put away a few spices and wipe down the counter. (And maybe listen to some music while you're at it?) Soon enough you'll find yourself in the flow of cooking, with clean counters to spare.

Shop strategically.

Key ingredients. I'm not a fan of buying food that *may* be used. A fully stocked fridge and pantry is a recipe for food waste. Instead, consider using the storage space for frequently used ingredients. For me, the list includes a few of my favorite spices, peeled garlic cloves, lemon juice, plain Greek yogurt, green onions, pre-cooked grains, and a few cans of beans. Note your own dinner staples so you can keep a back-up team of ingredients on repeat.

Grocery list apps. I'm here to relay that applying a bit of technology to food gathering has saved me many texts, grocery runs, and impulse food buys. Apps are an easy way to keep an updated grocery list on hand at all times — ones that sync across my computer, my phone, and my husband's phone. When it comes time for weekly grocery shopping, Josiah and I can truly divide and conquer without ripping a sheet of paper in half.

Keep non-dairy options handy.

Nutritional yeast. People are always asking me for tips on how to veganize meals. Swapping fortified nutritional yeast for grated cheese is among the easiest. It adds a nice cheesy creaminess to dishes, along with lots of vitamin B, including B-12, which can be in short supply when you don't eat animal products.

Plant-based milk. Switching to non-dairy milk was perhaps the easiest decision I made on the path to plant-based eating — there are just so many good options. A few of the following recipes ask for milk. Use only unsweetened, unflavored plant milk and steer clear of coconut milk — unless the recipe states otherwise — which can overpower other flavors.

Vegan cheese. Vegan options have multiplied in recent years and most of the cheeses I've tasted melt nicely and are delicious. Feel free to replace every cheese ingredient in my recipes with a non-dairy option.

I used to think one-pot cooking was about minimizing clean-up. But while that's certainly the case, the benefits don't stop there. Cooking in one pot lets you experience the crispiness of vegetables roasted on a sheet pan, the rich flavor of noodles marinated in a pot of vegetable juices, and the versatility of a stir fry flash-cooked in a skillet. I'm also one of those who struggles to time my cooking so everything's hot and ready to go at once. Not a problem if you're only focusing on the action in a single pot.

Before choosing a recipe, I suggest first reading it through so you can consider what you have on hand and how long it takes from prep to table. Take note of which ingredients need chopping or prepping, and handle that first. Julia Child's oft-quoted reassurance, "If you can read you can cook," applies here.

The following tips can help you make the most of whatever one-pot you choose to cook in.

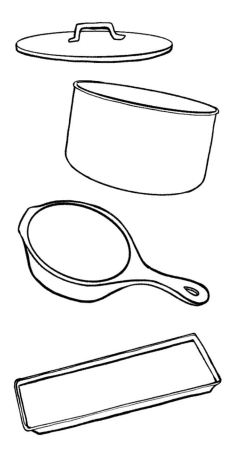

Stock pots: I like my stock pot, or soup pot, with a lid so it can generate heat while conserving liquids. Noodles and grains are more nutritious when cooked with vegetable juices in a single pot rather than added at the end, and vegetables more flavorful when they have time to marinate together. Stirring or adding a little more broth, water, or olive oil can prevent ingredients from drying out and sticking to the bottom, and turn stews into soups.

Skillets: I generally use a 12-inch skillet with a lid so I can better control the cooking process. A smaller skillet can crowd vegetables, making it harder to cook them evenly. You'll need a bigger skillet if you're cooking for a crowd. Heat a little oil in the pan before tossing in vegetables to quickly cook and help preserve their color and crispness. Sauté, or stir over heat, until the vegetables are just tender to the fork — the goal is to avoid overcooking them.

Sheet pans: I recommend using cookie sheets with a rim of one-inch (or so). Exactly where you place your ingredients on the pan is important. Vegetables on the outside tend to cook more quickly than those in the middle; if you want evenly cooked ingredients, place the larger slower-cooking pieces on the edges. For crispy vegetables, spread them out so more sides are exposed.

A couple more things: Not every recipe adheres strictly to the one-pot rule. Sometimes it's just easier to mix seasonings in a bowl rather than adding them one at a time to a sheet pan-full of vegetables — though it does go faster if you use your hands. A number of recipes call for cooked grains, which means another pot — unless you make up a big batch to use all week or buy grains pre-cooked, as I often do. And bear in mind that serving suggestions are just that — suggestions. Run with them, or choose to top off your dish with ingredients more to your liking. In short, jump on in and make these recipes your own. They're here for you.

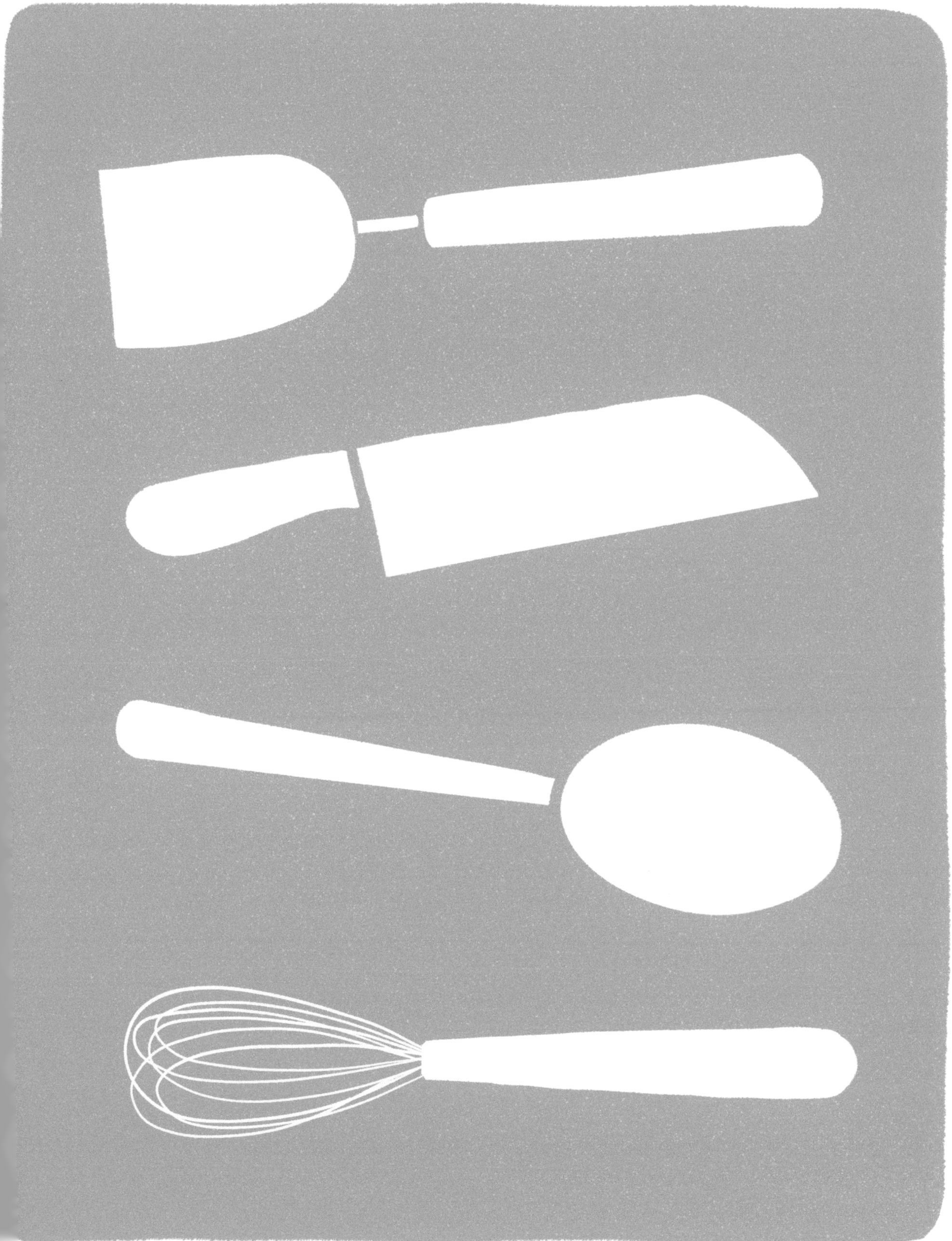

BAKED CAULIFLOWER with OLIVES, CHEESE & FENNEL SEEDS

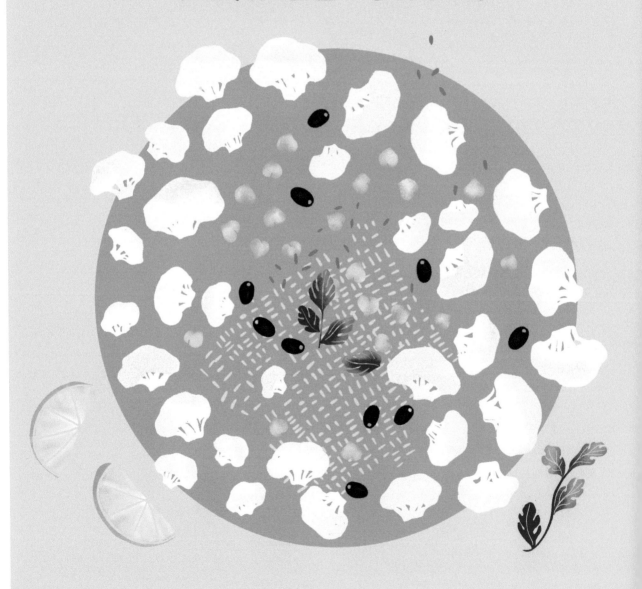

Baked Cauliflower with Olives, Cheese and Fennel Seeds

Prep to table: 45 minutes | Serves: 4

Roasted cauliflower is an easy win when it comes to dinner. It's good on its own with a little oil and seasoning, and gets even better when tossed with pitted olives and finished with melted Gruyere cheese. Go ahead and experiment with a variety of cheeses, or swap in nutritional yeast, which has the cheesy attitude that works fine here. This recipe calls for a two-stage roasting approach. Progressive roasting locks in the flavors and prevents the cheese from becoming too crispy — worth the outrageous effort of setting a timer on your phone for 20 minutes twice.

1 medium or large cauliflower, chopped

1 (15-ounce) can chickpeas, drained and rinsed

¼ cup olive oil

½ teaspoon salt, plus more to taste

2 teaspoons fennel seeds

6 garlic cloves, chopped

½ chopped pitted Kalamata olives

½ teaspoon red pepper flakes

½ cup grated Gruyere

Freshly ground black pepper

Serving suggestion: ½ cup chopped fresh parsley / 1 lemon, cut into wedges

1. **Preheat** the oven to 425 degrees. Toss together the cauliflower, chickpeas, olive oil, and ½ tsp of salt on a sheet pan. Roast for 20 minutes.

2. **Remove** the sheet pan from the oven. Add the fennel seeds, garlic, olives, and red pepper flakes and toss until combined. Sprinkle on the grated Gruyere and roast for another 20 minutes or until the cheese is slightly crispy but still melty.

3. **Season** with another sprinkling of salt and black pepper and serve in bowls. Top with parsley and a side of lemon wedges for squeezing.

Easy ingredient swaps: Caraway seeds for the fennel seeds / Chopped pitted green olives for the Kalamata olives / Chopped fresh mint or cilantro for the fresh parsley

Baked
SWEET POTATO
ENCHILADAS

Baked Sweet Potato Enchiladas

Prep to table: 60 to 75 minutes I Serves: 4

Close to our publication date, one of our recipe testers reached out to make sure this dinner had made the cut. It's a dish that her husband, whom she's dubbed The Reluctant Vegetarian, asks for over and over again. Flavorful, nourishing and so very simple, this recipe is completely in keeping with the spirit of *One & Done*, that is, healthy cooking does not have to be hard. This recipe combines spicy sauce with gooey baked sweet potatoes to recreate the familiar enchilada experience. Serve it with various toppings on the side so everyone can build the sweet potato enchilada of their dreams.

4 medium sweet potatoes

1 (15-ounce) can red enchilada sauce

1 (15-ounce) can black beans, drained and rinsed

1 to 1 ½ cups shredded mozzarella cheese, plus more if needed

Serving suggestion: 2 limes, cut into wedges / Sour cream / 4 green onions, thinly sliced / Fresh cilantro, chopped / 2 avocados, sliced / Enchilada sauce

1. **Preheat** the oven to 400 degrees. Pierce each sweet potato a few times with a fork and place on a sheet pan. Roast for 45 minutes to 1 hour, or until soft when pierced with a fork. Remove from the oven.

2. **Cut** the potatoes in half lengthwise. Holding each sweet potato half by its tip, gently mash the insides with a fork.

3. **Top** each sweet potato half with enchilada sauce, a scoop of black beans, and a sprinkle of cheese, and roast for another 15 to 20 minutes or until the cheese is melted.

4. **Serve** with the toppings in individual bowls.

Easy ingredient swaps: Shredded cheddar cheese for the mozzarella / Plain Greek yogurt for the sour cream / Salsa for the enchilada sauce

crispy GARLIC POTATOES with MUSHROOMS & KALE

Crispy Garlic Potatoes with Mushrooms and Kale

Prep to table: 60 minutes | Serves: 4

Perhaps the best way to cook kale is on a sheet pan. It crisps up beautifully and tastes delicious — almost like healthy green potato chips. In fact, I often snack on them. When I want to eat kale chips for dinner I just add potatoes and mushrooms and watch them all roast. I recommend using Hot Tahini Sauce to pull it all together or just whisk together some tahini paste with a little water until it's thin enough to pour.

1 pound new potatoes, quartered

6 to 8 garlic cloves, chopped

1 tablespoon dried herbs de Provence

1 teaspoon salt, plus more if needed

3 tablespoons olive oil, divided

½ pound small mushrooms, sliced

4 cups stemmed and coarsely
   chopped kale

Serving suggestion: ½ cup Hot Tahini Sauce (p. 146) / Crispy chickpeas / Freshly ground black pepper

1. **Preheat** the oven to 425 degrees. Toss together the potatoes, garlic, herbs de Provence, salt, and 2 tablespoons of olive oil on a large sheet pan.

2. **Roast** for 25 minutes. Remove the sheet pan from the oven, and add the mushrooms, kale, and the remaining tablespoon of olive oil. Toss with a spatula until evenly coated.

3. **Roast** for another 25 minutes, or until the potatoes and kale are tender and crispy.

4. **Serve** with a little Hot Tahini Sauce, crispy chickpeas (available in most grocery stores), and a sprinkling of salt and black pepper.

Easy ingredient swaps: Dried rosemary for the herbs de Provence / Store bought pesto or Creamy Herb Sauce (p. 146) for the Hot Tahini Sauce

GOAT CHEESE & SUN-DRIED
— tomato-stuffed —
PORTOBELLO MUSHROOMS

Goat Cheese and Sun-Dried Tomato-Stuffed Portobello Mushrooms

Prep to table: 30 minutes | Serves: 4

These juicy stuffed portobello mushrooms finished off with a balsamic glaze are the answer to meaty cravings. My favorite way to eat this dish is on a bed of simply dressed greens. It also works as appetizers if you swap in small mushrooms for the big ones. While cooking the mushrooms, don't be alarmed if moisture begins to pool on the sheet pan. It's normal and doesn't mean they'll be soggy. The balsamic glaze, thicker and sweeter than balsamic vinegar, adds an essential richness. I rely on store bought balsamic glaze since I don't love stirring vinegar and sugar over a hot stove. You can generally find it in grocery stores next to the balsamic vinegar.

8 medium to large portobello mushrooms, stems removed

2 tablespoons olive oil

4 garlic cloves, minced

¾ teaspoon salt, plus more to taste

1 to 2 cups arugula

1 cup crumbled goat cheese

2 tablespoons chopped sun-dried tomatoes

1 cup chopped nuts (roasted pine and almonds, or plain walnuts), plus more for topping

½ teaspoon freshly ground black pepper

2 tablespoons balsamic glaze

Serving suggestion: Fresh arugula / Nuts / Fresh parsley, chopped

1. **Preheat** the oven to 400 degrees. Coat the mushrooms with 2 tablespoons of oil and place them, stem side up, on a large sheet pan. Sprinkle mushrooms with the garlic and salt.

2. **Roast** for 9 minutes. Carefully flip over the mushrooms and bake for another 9 minutes.

3. **Remove** from the oven. Using a cutting board, roughly chop the arugula. Mix in the goat cheese, sun-dried tomatoes, nuts, and black pepper. Stuff each mushroom cap with the mixture and drizzle on a little balsamic glaze. Bake for 6 more minutes, or until the cheese is melty.

4. **Serve** over a bed of fresh arugula and top with more nuts and parsley.

Easy ingredient swaps: Roughly chopped spinach for the arugula / Chunky medium salsa for the sun-dried tomatoes

PORTOBELLO
MUSHROOM PARMIGIANA

Portobello Mushroom Parmigiana

Prep to table: 30 minutes | Serves: 3 to 4

I've swapped mushrooms for eggplant in this delicious and easy parmigiana. One mushroom is typically a full serving, but throw on another if you're hungry. While the mushrooms, roasted cherry tomatoes, and melted mozzarella can hold their own, the crispy bread crumb topping is the part that makes me want to blow a chef's kiss and say *benissimo*!

1 cup halved cherry tomatoes

6 medium to large portobello mushrooms,
   stems removed

6 garlic cloves, minced

4 tablespoons olive oil

Salt

Freshly ground black pepper

Pesto sauce (optional)

6 tablespoons chunky salsa

1 cup shredded mozzarella

½ cup panko bread crumbs

Serving suggestion: Salad greens, lightly dressed / Chopped fresh basil

1. **Preheat** the oven to 425 degrees. Line a sheet pan with parchment paper. Toss together the cherry tomatoes, mushrooms, garlic, and olive oil on the pan and season with salt and pepper.

2. **Brush** the insides of the mushrooms with pesto sauce, if you want to enhance the flavors. Arrange them on the pan, stem side up, and fill each with 1 tablespoon of salsa. Top with the mozzarella cheese and bread crumbs.

3. **Roast** for 15 to 20 minutes, or until the cheese is melted and the bread crumbs are toasted.

4. **Serve** the mushrooms on lightly dressed greens with the tomatoes and chopped basil on top.

Easy ingredient swaps: Tomato paste for the salsa

COCONUT & GINGER
THAI CURRY
— WITH SPINACH —

Coconut and Ginger Thai Curry with Spinach

Prep to table: 30 minutes | Serves: 4

This colorful take on Thai curry features pops of red and green from the cherry tomatoes and spinach. But the fresh spicy ginger — and golden color — is what most people remark on. Once you've got the hang of this recipe, go ahead and introduce different vegetables — zucchini, leeks, broccoli, and eggplant would work nicely here. Serve it as is, or over your favorite rice.

2 tablespoons olive oil

1 medium yellow onion, chopped

6 garlic cloves, chopped

1½-inch piece (1½ tablespoons) fresh ginger, grated

1 small red or green bell pepper, chopped

1 small carrot, peeled, chopped

1 teaspoon salt, divided, plus more if needed

1 teaspoon freshly ground black pepper, divided, plus more if needed

4 teaspoons curry powder

¼ teaspoon red pepper flakes

1 (13.5-ounce) can light coconut milk

1 cup vegetable broth

½ cup halved cherry tomatoes

2 cups packed fresh spinach

Serving suggestion: 3 to 4 cups cooked rice / Unsweetened dry coconut / ½ to ¾ cup roasted slivered almonds

1. **Heat** the olive oil in a large pot over medium heat. Add the onion, garlic, ginger, peppers, carrots, ½ teaspoon of salt, and ½ teaspoon of black pepper, and cook, stirring often, until softened, 5 to 7 minutes.

2. **Add** the curry powder, red pepper flakes, coconut milk, vegetable broth, and the remaining ½ teaspoon of salt and ½ teaspoon of black pepper. Decrease the heat slightly and cook, stirring often, for 10 minutes.

3. **Stir** in the tomatoes and spinach and cook for another 5 minutes. Taste and season with salt and pepper as needed.

4. **Serve** on bowls of rice topped with coconut flakes and a sprinkling of nuts.

Easy ingredient swaps: 1 teaspoon ground ginger for the fresh grated ginger / Broccoli for the peppers and/or carrots / Cumin for the curry powder / 1 cup snow peas for the spinach / Almond or cashew milk (unflavored, unsweetened) for the coconut milk

GOLDEN CARROT & CURRY SOUP

Golden Carrot and Curry Soup

Prep to table: 35 minutes | Serves 4

This carrot soup is one that looks good and is good for you. Loaded with beta carotene, it includes protein, too, and the generous helping of greens is your permission to confidently decline that side salad. If you want to play with the recipe, swap in coconut oil for the olive oil and light coconut milk for the plant-based milk for a mild coconut-y flavor.

2 tablespoons olive oil

1 medium yellow onion, chopped

1 medium sweet potato, peeled, chopped

3 large carrots, sliced

1 ½ teaspoons salt, divided

5 garlic cloves, minced

2 tablespoons curry powder

½ teaspoon ground cinnamon

1-inch piece (1 tablespoon) fresh ginger, grated

5 cups vegetable broth

¾ cup lentils, rinsed

½ cup unsweetened, unflavored plant-based milk (almond, cashew or soy)

½ teaspoon freshly ground black pepper

1 squeeze lemon juice

2 to 3 cups packed chopped fresh spinach

Serving suggestion: Toasted pumpkin seeds

1. **Sauté** the oil, onion, sweet potato, carrots, and 1 teaspoon salt in a large soup pot over medium heat for 8 minutes**.** Add the garlic, curry, cinnamon, and ginger and sauté for 1 more minute.

2. **Add** the broth, lentils, and the remaining ½ teaspoon salt and bring to a boil over high heat. Lower the heat and simmer until the sweet potatoes and carrots are soft, about 20 minutes.

3. **Stir** in the plant-based milk. Taste and add salt, black pepper, and a squeeze of lemon juice.

4. **Add** the spinach, one handful at a time, and stir until it wilts, about 1 minute. Use an immersion blender to get the consistency you want.

5. **Serve** topped with a sprinkle of toasted pumpkin seeds.

Easy ingredient swaps: Coconut oil for the olive oil / 1 cup chopped butternut squash for the sweet potato / Light coconut milk for the plant-based milk / Chopped and stemmed kale or collard greens for the spinach

PITA STUFFED *with* MIDDLE EASTERN-SPICED CAULIFLOWER & BLACK OLIVES

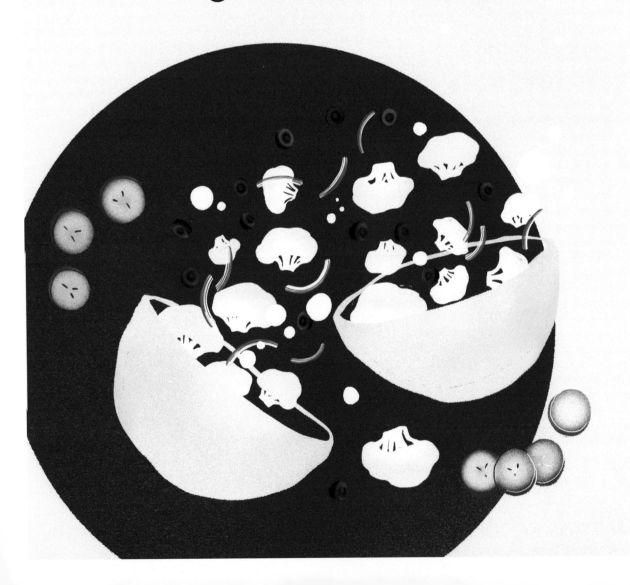

Pita Stuffed with Middle Eastern-Spiced Cauliflower and Black Olives

Prep to table: 45 minutes | Serves 4

This recipe draws on classic Middle Eastern spices to make cauliflower, red onion, and black olives the yummy filling in a toasted pita sandwich. What I like best about this dish is the chance to stuff your pita any number of ways. I've suggested a few options, like black olives and halved cherry tomatoes, to help get you started. All the stuffing options make this a dish that plays well with a crowd.

4 tablespoons olive oil

1 ½ teaspoons ground cumin

2 teaspoons paprika

1 teaspoon salt

1 teaspoon ground coriander

1 teaspoon ground turmeric

4 garlic cloves, minced

1 medium cauliflower, chopped

1 red onion, thinly chopped

4 small pita breads, toasted (or 2 large)

Serving suggestion: 1 medium cucumber, thinly sliced / 1 cup black Kalamata olives, pitted and halved / 1 cup halved cherry tomatoes / 1 cup baba ganoush / ½ cup hummus / Creamy Herb Sauce (p. 146)

1. **Preheat** the oven to 425 degrees. Mix together on a sheet pan the cauliflower, red onion, olive oil, cumin, paprika, salt, coriander, turmeric, and garlic. Toss with your hands until well coated, then spread it all out in a single layer.

2. **Roast** for 30 to 40 minutes, or until the cauliflower is slightly crisp and golden brown.

3. **Slice** the pita breads in half, and toast them. Stuff with the cauliflower and red onion mixture.

4. **Serve** with bowls of thinly sliced cucumber, black olives, cherry tomatoes, baba ganoush, hummus, and Creamy Herb Sauce.

Easy ingredient swap: Sweet potato instead of cauliflower for a sweeter option / Hot Tahini Sauce (p. 146) or tahini paste thinned with water, so it's sauce-like, for the Creamy Herb Sauce

ROASTED CAULIFLOWER
& RED ONION TACOS *with guacamole*

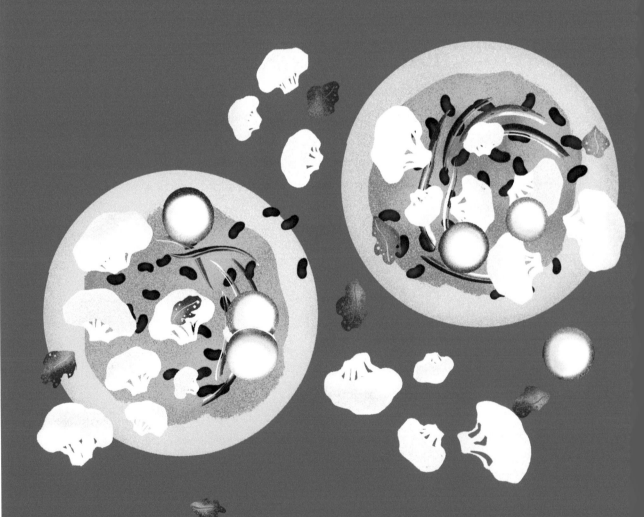

Roasted Cauliflower and Red Onion Tacos with Guacamole

Prep to table: 45 minutes I Serves 4

Cauliflower is popular for a reason: it's super healthy, versatile, and so mild it easily absorbs flavors. Here, it holds down tacos with the help of red onions, garlic and other seasonings, along with guacamole and plenty of toppings. I like to up the protein content by adding black beans but it's all good if you want to go pure guac and cauli. To warm the tortillas: Cover three or four of them on a plate with a damp paper towel and microwave for 30 seconds. They'll stay moist and flexible.

1 medium cauliflower, chopped

1 large red onion, sliced or chopped

3 tablespoons olive oil

8 garlic cloves, minced

2 teaspoons ground cumin

1 teaspoon ground coriander

Heavy dash of cayenne or red pepper flakes

½ to 1 teaspoon salt

Serving suggestion: 8 (6-inch) corn tortillas / 1 (16-ounce) can black beans, drained and rinsed / 1 to 1 ½ cups guacamole, store bought or homemade / ½ cup thinly sliced radishes / ½ cup chopped cilantro / ½ cup shredded cheese of your choice / Tortilla chips

1. **Preheat** the oven to 400 degrees. Toss the cauliflower, red onion, olive oil, garlic, cumin, coriander, cayenne, and salt on a sheet pan, until everything is evenly coated.

2. **Roast** for 25 to 35 minutes, or until the cauliflower is slightly brown on the edges.

3. **Warm** the black beans and tortillas just before serving.

4. **Serve** the roasted cauliflower and red onion in warm tortillas with bowls of the beans, guacamole, and toppings of your choice on the side.

Easy ingredient swaps: Broccoli for the cauliflower / Lentils or refried pinto beans for the black beans / Sliced avocados for the guacamole

ROASTED RED BELL PEPPER & AVOCADO TOSTADAS

Roasted Red Bell Pepper and Avocado Tostadas

Prep to table: 15 to 30 minutes I Serves 2 to 3

Tostadas are essentially open-faced tortillas made of flour or corn. In this recipe, they're the crispy plat-form for refried beans topped with sweet-savory roasted red peppers and avocados. Not surprisingly, the brand of refried beans used makes a difference. Our testing team liked *Amy's Organic Traditional Refried Beans* and *Goya Organics Refried Black Beans (Vegan)*. You can buy tostadas or, to make your own, lightly oil a sheet pan, space out corn or flour tortillas, and bake for 10 minutes until crispy, flipping them halfway through.

2 red bell peppers, seeded, chopped

1 yellow onion, chopped

1 to 2 tablespoons olive oil

½ teaspoon salt

1 teaspoon ground cumin

1 teaspoon chili powder

3 garlic cloves, minced

4 to 6 tostada shells

1 (15-ounce) can refried beans (vegan)

Serving suggestion: Radishes, thinly sliced / 1 to 2 avocados, chopped / Feta cheese, crumbled / Salsa / ½ to ¾ cup chopped fresh cilantro / 1 lime, cut into wedges

1. **Preheat** the oven to 400 degrees. Coat the peppers and onion in olive oil, salt, cumin, chili powder, and garlic and roast for 20 to 30 minutes, or until soft. If strapped for time, sauté the peppers, onion, and seasonings for 5 to 8 minutes in a skillet instead of roasting, and you'll be ready to eat in 15 minutes or less.

2. **Transfer** the vegetables to paper towels, and wipe the pan clean.

3. **Place** the tostada shells on the sheet pan, spread on a thick layer of refried beans, and top with the roasted red peppers and onion. Return to the oven until the beans and shells are warm, about 5 minutes.

4. **Serve** with avocados, cheese, salsa, cilantro, and lime wedges.

Easy ingredient swaps: Any hard shredded cheese for the feta / Parsley for the cilantro / Lemon wedges for the lime

balsamic BRUSSELS SPROUTS
— AND FIGS —

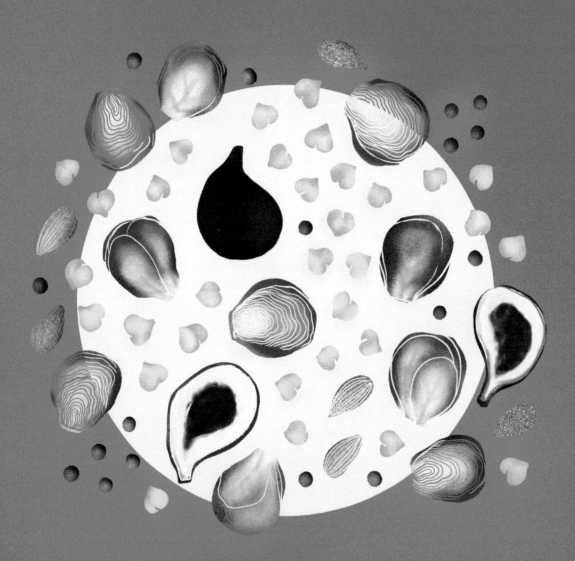

Balsamic Brussels Sprouts and Figs

Prep to table: 40 minutes | Serves: 4

Brussels sprouts have become the new French fry — crispy and verging on addictive when properly roasted. In this recipe, they're cooked with balsamic vinegar, a touch of maple syrup, and dried figs. Capers deliver the salty punch. I like my sprouts on a bed of grains, sometimes doused with a little Mint Yogurt Sauce.

4 cups trimmed and halved Brussels sprouts

1 (15-ounce) can chickpeas, drained and rinsed

3 tablespoons olive oil

4 garlic cloves, minced

1 teaspoon salt

2 teaspoons maple syrup

3 tablespoons balsamic vinegar

2 tablespoons capers, drained

6 dried figs, stems removed and quartered

Serving suggestion: Cooked quinoa / ½ cup chopped roasted almonds / Mint Yogurt Sauce (p. 146)

1. **Preheat** the oven to 425 degrees. Toss together the Brussels sprouts, chickpeas, olive oil, garlic, salt, and maple syrup on a sheet pan, and roast for 25 to 30 minutes, or until crispy. Let sit on a wire rack.

2. **Add** the balsamic vinegar, capers, and figs and toss until combined.

3. **Serve** as is, or on a cooked grain, like quinoa. Top with roasted almonds and the Mint Yogurt Sauce.

Easy ingredient swaps: Honey or brown sugar for the maple syrup—or just leave it out if you'd like something less sweet / ½ cup shredded Parmesan cheese for the capers / ½ cup dried cranberries for the figs / White or brown rice for the quinoa / A vinaigrette dressing for the Mint Yogurt Sauce

garlic-flavored MUSHROOMS & SPINACH with BAKED FETA

Garlic-Flavored Mushrooms and Spinach with Baked Feta

Prep to table: 30 minutes | Serves: 3 to 4

A standout feature of this sheet-pan meal is the way baked feta tastes, especially when nestled into crispy garlic-flavored spinach and roasted mushrooms. Another option is to use halloumi cheese, or even firm tofu, if you want to skip the dairy. I love the addition of sesame seeds here, which add crunch and nuttiness. Buy the seeds toasted or, to toast them yourself: Heat the seeds without any oil in a small skillet, stirring until lightly browned.

1 pound small mushrooms, sliced

1 large red or yellow onion, thinly sliced

8 garlic cloves, peeled and quartered

4 to 6 cups fresh spinach

3 tablespoons olive oil, plus more to taste

4 to 6 ounces feta cheese, cut into ½-inch slices

Salt

Freshly ground black pepper

4 tablespoons toasted sesame seeds

Serving suggestion: 3 to 4 cups cooked brown rice, farro, or polenta / Sriracha

1. **Preheat** the oven to 425 degrees. Line a sheet pan with parchment paper. On the pan, toss together the mushrooms, onion, garlic, spinach, and oil. Add the feta and make sure the slices touch the paper so they crisp up. Season with salt and black pepper.

2. **Roast** for 20 minutes, or until the mushrooms are lightly browned. Use a spatula to stir the vegetables once or twice, so they cook more evenly. For crispier spinach, continue to roast until it's lightly browned.

3. **Remove** the pan from the oven and sprinkle the spinach, feta, and mushrooms with toasted sesame seeds.

4. **Serve** as is, or on a bed of grains, with sriracha if you want more heat.

Easy ingredient swaps: Halloumi cheese or firm tofu for the feta cheese / Roasted sunflower seeds for the sesame seeds

Italian TOMATOES, WHITE BEANS and GREENS with FARRO

Italian Tomatoes, White Beans and Greens with Farro

Prep to table: 40 minutes | Serves: 4

This dish is among my favorites. Not only is it beautiful, with its vivid combination of red tomatoes, white beans, and vibrant greens. But for a dish I'd serve at a dinner party, it's absurdly easy to pull together — an exception to the too-good-to-be-true rule. The farro, a type of high-protein, high-fiber whole-grain wheat, lends a pleasantly chewy texture to this dish. To prevent it from sticking to the pan, stir in olive oil towards the end of the cooking process. Use fresh cherry tomatoes if you can, but canned diced tomatoes also work. Serve this hearty Italian dish in rustic ceramic bowls and top off with pesto sauce and chopped fresh basil. *Buon appetito!*

2 cups vegetable broth

1 cup farro

2 cups cherry tomatoes, halved (about 1 pint)

1 leek, thinly sliced

4 garlic cloves, minced

1 teaspoon salt, plus more if needed

2 cups stemmed and chopped kale

1 teaspoon Italian seasoning

1 (15-ounce) can butter beans, drained and rinsed

2 tablespoons olive oil

Freshly ground black pepper

Serving suggestion: 4 teaspoons pesto sauce / Grated Parmesan cheese / Chopped fresh basil

1. **Bring** the vegetable broth, farro, tomatoes, leek, garlic, and salt to a boil in a medium-sized pot over high heat. Lower the heat to medium-low, and simmer for about 15 minutes.

2. **Add** the kale, Italian seasoning, and butter beans. Partially cover the pot and continue to simmer until the liquid has been absorbed and the farro is cooked, about 15 minutes. Add more water or broth as needed to keep it from drying out.

3. **Stir** in the olive oil, scraping up the bottom with the spoon so the farro mixture doesn't stick. Season with additional salt and black pepper to taste.

4. **Spoon** the mixture into bowls and top with pesto sauce, grated Parmesan cheese, and chopped basil.

Easy ingredient swaps: 1 can (14-ounces) diced tomatoes for the cherry tomatoes / ½ yellow onion, chopped, for the leek / Fresh spinach or frozen spinach (8 ounces) for the kale / Herbs de Provence for the Italian seasoning / Any white bean for the butter beans / Nutritional yeast for the grated parmesan / Creamy Herb Yogurt Sauce (p. 146) for the pesto

KIP'S RICH MUSHROOM
Risotto

Kip's Rich Mushroom Risotto

Prep to table: 30 minutes | Serves: 4

While recipes for mushroom risotto abound, this is Kip's favorite. Who's Kip? He's married to Clare, my publisher, and is a really good cook. Kip started cooking risotto about 20 years ago and does it mostly "by feel" these days. He often makes this dish for friends accustomed to eating meat — with this risotto, no one misses it. He adds dried mushrooms to the vegetable broth to give the rice the umami richness you typically get from beef or veal stock. He also recommends using saltier cheeses, like Parmesan or a good aged Gouda, over milder cheeses. I've had the risotto with and without a drizzle of truffle oil — both ways are delicious.

4 cups vegetable broth

1 package (1- to 2-ounces) dried mushrooms, porcini or mixed

3 tablespoons olive oil, divided

1 yellow onion, roughly chopped

4 to 5 medium-large portobello mushrooms, cut into ½ inch cubes

Salt

Freshly ground black pepper

Dried or fresh thyme

$2/3$ cup arborio rice

1 cup fresh basil, cut into strips, divided

$2/3$ cup grated cheese, such as Parmesan or aged Gouda, plus more for garnish

Serving suggestion: Fresh basil, cut into strips / 1 tablespoon truffle oil

1. **Microwave** the vegetable broth in a large measuring cup for 1 minute. Add the dried mushrooms and let sit for 30 minutes.

2. **Heat** 2 tablespoons of the oil in a 12-inch skillet over medium heat. Add the onions and half the mushrooms. Season with dashes of salt, black pepper, and thyme, and sauté until the liquid released by the mushrooms dries up and they're seared, or lightly browned, about 10 minutes. Transfer to a plate. Repeat with the remaining mushrooms.

3. **Add** the remaining 1 tablespoon of olive oil to the same skillet with the arborio rice and cook, stirring constantly, for 1 to 2 minutes.

4. **Pour** about ½ cup of the vegetable broth and mushroom mixture into the skillet and cook, stirring, until almost all the liquid has evaporated. Repeat until the rice is *al dente*, which means cooked but firm to the bite.

5. **Add** the mushroom and onion mixture to the rice and stir until combined. Mix in $2/3$ cup of the basil along with the cheese. Continue to stir the risotto over heat until it's the consistency of oatmeal, about 2 to 3 minutes. Add more broth, if needed.

6. **Serve** the risotto topped with the remaining basil and a little truffle oil.

MISO GLAZED
Cabbage AND WALNUTS
WITH POLENTA

Miso Glazed Cabbage and Walnuts with Polenta

Prep to table: 25 minutes | Serves 4

Long a staple of plant-based eating because it's a healthy food with satisfying crunch, cabbage got an extra boost during the pandemic because it also keeps well in a fridge. For those reasons, and more, we bring you cabbage cooked with toasted walnuts and miso, a fermented soybean paste that lends a sweet-savory umami flavor to foods. Yum. When it comes to miso paste, choose your own adventure. White, or shiro, miso is the most adaptable. Yellow is also mild, but fermented a little longer than white. Red miso, the saltiest, can sometimes overwhelm milder flavors but that intensity is also why so many like it.

1 cup walnut pieces

2 tablespoons light, or untoasted, sesame oil

2 tablespoons red miso paste

4 garlic cloves, minced

4 green onions, thinly sliced, divided

2 teaspoons soy sauce

1 tablespoon maple syrup

1 tablespoon lime juice

2 tablespoons rice vinegar

1 small head green or red cabbage,
  sliced, roughly chopped

½ cup chopped fresh mint

Freshly ground black pepper

Serving suggestion: Cooked polenta

1. **Roast** the walnut pieces in a large unoiled pot over medium heat until the nuts are lightly browned, stirring occasionally, for about 3 to 5 minutes. When done, transfer to a paper towel.

2. **Heat** the sesame oil in the same large pot over medium heat for 2 minutes.

3. **Turn** off the heat and stir in the miso paste, garlic, 3 chopped green onions, soy sauce, maple syrup, lime juice, and rice vinegar.

4. **Turn** the heat to medium, add the cabbage and sauté, or stir over heat, until it becomes crisp-tender and browned, 8 to 10 minutes.

5. **Add** the walnuts and mint, season with black pepper, and stir for 1 minute until well combined.

6. **Serve** over warm polenta and top with the remaining green onions.

Easy ingredient swaps: Roasted cashews or almonds for the walnuts / Olive oil for the sesame oil / 2 tablespoons capers for the miso paste / Brown sugar for the maple syrup / Lemon juice for the lime juice / Parsley for the mint / Brown rice for the polenta

ROASTED CUMIN CARROTS with FRESH MINT & COUSCOUS

Roasted Cumin Carrots with Fresh Mint and Couscous

Prep to table: 40 minutes | Serves: 4

One of the easiest ways to appreciate carrots is by roasting them. Add a little oil, salt, and pepper and they're delicious. But an entrée deserves more, so I introduced chickpeas along with cumin and corian-der, the dream team of spices, and some mint. Mint's fresh taste makes the dish more of a sit-up-and-pay-attention experience — one worth sharing with others. If your in-laws, new neighbors, or someone else you're trying to *wow* accepts your dinner invitation, thrill them with rainbow carrots as well.

12 medium carrots, peeled, cut into
   1-inch chunks
1 (16-ounce) can chickpeas, drained and rinsed
4 tablespoons olive oil

1 ½ teaspoons ground cumin
1 ½ teaspoons ground coriander
½ teaspoon salt
½ teaspoon freshly ground black pepper

Serving suggestion: 3 to 4 cups cooked couscous / 1 cup Lemon Tahini Sauce (p. 146) / ¼ cup chopped fresh mint leaves / ½ cup finely chopped red onion / Shelled roasted pistachios

1. **Preheat** the oven to 400 degrees. Toss the carrots, chickpeas, olive oil, cumin, coriander, salt, and black pepper on a sheet pan until evenly coated.

2. **Roast** for 25 to 35 minutes, or until the carrots are soft when pierced with a fork, and the chickpeas turn light brown. Remove from the oven, and season with salt and pepper to taste.

3. **Serve** over couscous. Top with the Lemon Tahini Sauce, fresh mint, red onions, and nuts.

Easy ingredient swaps: Ground ginger for the coriander / Brown rice or salad greens for the couscous / Mint Yogurt Sauce (p. 146) or your own variation on herbs and plain yogurt for the Lemon Tahini Sauce / Roasted almonds or raw walnut pieces for the pistachios

SPICY LENTILS
WITH RICE & greens

Spicy Lentils with Rice and Greens

Prep to table: 35 minutes | Serves 4

I've long thought lentils don't get the respect they deserve. They pack lots of protein, efficiently absorb the flavor of whatever they're cooked with, and need zero amount of soaking. (Experts do recommend rinsing them in a colander before cooking to remove any dust and debris.) In this dish, inspired by a traditional Middle Eastern recipe called mujadara, they get their due. In addition to mujadara's traditional lentils, onion, and herbs, I've added a generous helping of greens. Serve this dish as is, or with Creamy Herb Sauce or a dollop of plain Greek yogurt to cool the bold spices and add a creamy flourish. (I'm beginning to question if there is anything that is not enhanced with a dollop of yogurt. Existential questions for a later time.)

3 tablespoons olive oil	½ teaspoon ground nutmeg
1 medium yellow onion, chopped	½ teaspoon red pepper flakes (optional)
1 ½ teaspoons salt, divided, plus more to taste	4 cups water
5 garlic cloves, minced	1 cup brown or green lentils, rinsed
¾ cup brown rice	4 cups stemmed and chopped kale
1 ½ teaspoons ground cumin	

Serving suggestion: Creamy Herb Sauce (p. 146) / Toasted almonds / Lemon wedges

1. **Warm** the olive oil in a large pot over medium heat. Add the onion and ½ teaspoon of the salt and cook, stirring often, until the onions are translucent and fragrant, about 3 to 4 minutes.

2. **Add** the garlic and cook for 1 more minute.

3. **Stir** in the rice, cumin, nutmeg, and red pepper flakes, if you want more heat, and cook for 1 more minute.

4. **Add** the water, lentils, and remaining 1 teaspoon of salt. Cover and cook, stirring occasionally, until the water has been absorbed and the lentils and rice are cooked through, 15 to 20 minutes. Add a little water if the lentils and rice are drying up and need further cooking.

5. **Remove** the pot from the heat, and stir in the kale until wilted.

6. **Serve** with Creamy Herb Sauce, a sprinkling of toasted almonds, and lemon wedges.

Easy ingredient swaps: 1 large leek, sliced, for the yellow onion / Spinach or arugula for the kale / Chopped roasted cashews or pistachios for the almonds / Plain Greek yogurt for the Creamy Herb Sauce

braised
MUSHROOM, PEPPER
& TOMATO CACCIATORE

Braised Mushroom, Pepper and Tomato Cacciatore

Prep to table: 45 minutes | Serves 4 to 6

Braising is a simple technique of pan-searing and then slowly cooking vegetables or meat covered in liquid. In this pasta dish, the technique makes the mushrooms, peppers, and tomatoes more flavorful by giving them extra stewing time. Throw in the noodles along with everything else and they soak up the garlic and vegetable flavors as they soften.

2 tablespoons olive oil

1 medium yellow onion, chopped

½ pound cremini or white mushrooms, sliced

1 red bell pepper, seeded, chopped

½ teaspoon salt

3 tablespoons capers

¼ cup pitted, chopped Kalamata olives

4 tablespoons salsa

4 garlic cloves, minced

1 teaspoon dried rosemary

1 tablespoon red wine vinegar

¾ teaspoon freshly ground black pepper

1 (14-ounce) can diced tomatoes, with juice

6 ounces short pasta, such as fusilli or farfalle

½ cup chopped fresh basil

Serving suggestion: ¼ teaspoon red pepper flakes / Olive oil / Grated Parmesan

1. **Warm** the olive oil in a large pot over medium heat. Add the onion, mushrooms, bell pepper, and salt and sauté until fragrant, about 6 minutes.

2. **Stir** in the capers, olives, salsa, garlic, and rosemary and continue to cook for about 3 more minutes. Add the red wine vinegar and black pepper and sauté for another 3 minutes.

3. **Add** the diced tomatoes, pasta, and 1 ½ cups water and bring to a boil. Partially cover the pot, lower the heat to medium-low and simmer, stirring occasionally to keep the pasta from sticking to the bottom of the pan, until the pasta is cooked, about 20 minutes. Add up to ¼ cup of water if the mixture starts drying out.

4. **Add** the basil about 5 minutes before the pasta is cooked through, and season with red pepper flakes. Finish with a drizzle of olive oil and a sprinkle of Parmesan cheese.

Easy ingredient swaps: Black olives for the Kalamata olives / Tomato paste for the salsa / Herbs de Provence or oregano for the rosemary / Chopped fresh cilantro or parsley instead of the basil / Nutritional yeast for the Parmesan

CHERRY TOMATO & OLIVE PASTA WITH lemon zest

Cherry Tomato and Olive Pasta with Lemon Zest

Prep to table: 30 minutes | Serves: 4

This pasta dish is the picture of one-pot elegance and grace, by which I mean it's beautiful enough to serve at one of your dinner parties. The noodles benefit from the all-in-one pot technique — they're more flavorful after being cooked with the other ingredients — and the lemon zest builds in brightness and depth. Lots of stirring is involved, especially toward the end, to keep the pasta from sticking to the bottom. On the plus side, you're breathing in the steamy fragrance of the garlic, paprika, and cumin. Toss in lots of parsley to accent this mostly red beauty of a dish.

4 tablespoons olive oil

1 medium yellow onion, chopped

2 cups halved cherry tomatoes

1 teaspoon salt, divided, plus more if needed

8 medium garlic cloves, chopped

2 teaspoons ground cumin

1 teaspoon paprika

2 ¾ cups vegetable broth

8 ounces short pasta, like farfalle or orecchiette

½ cup shaved Parmesan or Romano cheese

¾ cup chopped pitted green olives

½ teaspoon red pepper flakes, plus more if needed

1 tablespoon lemon zest

Freshly ground black pepper

Serving suggestion: 1 cup chopped parsley

1. **Sauté** the olive oil, onion, tomatoes, and ½ tsp of salt in a large soup pot over medium heat until fragrant, 5 to 6 minutes. Add the garlic, cumin, and paprika and sauté for 1 more minute.

2. **Stir** in the broth, pasta, and the remaining ½ teaspoon of salt and bring to a simmer over medium-low heat. Cover partially and cook until the broth is absorbed and the noodles just cooked, about 15 minutes. Stir occasionally to keep the ingredients from sticking to the bottom. If the pasta dries out before it's fully cooked, add a little more broth.

3. **Remove** the pot from the heat. Stir in the cheese, olives, red pepper flakes, and lemon zest. Taste, and season with salt and black pepper.

4. **Serve** sprinkled with fresh green parsley.

Easy ingredient swaps: Feta cheese for the Parmesan or Romano cheese / Pitted Kalamata olives or regular black olives, for the green olives / 1 tablespoon lemon juice for the zest / Fresh basil for the parsley

creamy MUSHROOM AND SPINACH PASTA

Creamy Mushroom and Spinach Pasta

Prep to table: 30 minutes | Serves: 4

I cook this pasta when I'm in the mood for something cozy. Maybe I've had a bad day at work. Maybe I just need to treat myself. But this creamy version of spinach and mushrooms, laced with B vitamin-rich nutritional yeast, generally makes me feel better. Pasta cooked with vegetables can sometimes resemble a bowl of stew, so I err on using a little less liquid. If the pasta starts drying up before it's fully cooked, add a little broth. For the plant-based milk, choose anything that's unflavored and unsweetened — except for coconut milk, which can be overwhelming here.

3 tablespoons olive oil, divided

1 medium yellow onion, thinly sliced

5 garlic cloves, minced

½ pound small mushrooms, sliced

1 tablespoon soy sauce

1 tablespoon lemon juice

1 teaspoon dried thyme

1 ¾ cups vegetable broth, plus more as needed

¾ cup unsweetened non-dairy milk

8 ounces short pasta, like orecchiette, elbow macaroni, or rotini

¾ teaspoon salt

2 to 4 cups fresh spinach

3 tablespoons nutritional yeast

Serving suggestion: Red pepper flakes

1. **Heat** 2 tablespoons of olive oil in a large pot over medium heat. Add the onion and sauté until fragrant, about 3 to 4 minutes. Add the garlic and sauté for another minute.

2. **Toss** in the mushrooms and soy sauce and cook until the mushrooms soften, another 3 to 5 minutes.

3. **Stir** in the lemon juice, freeing up any bits of onion, garlic, or mushrooms that might be stuck to the bottom of the pan.

4. **Add** the thyme, vegetable broth, non-dairy milk, pasta, and salt and bring to a boil.

5. **Lower** the heat to medium-low, partially cover the pot, and simmer until the pasta is cooked, about 10 to 12 minutes. Add broth if the pasta needs more liquid to fully cook.

6. **Stir** the fresh spinach and nutritional yeast into the cooked pasta until the spinach has wilted, about 1 minute.

7. **Turn** off the heat. Stir in the remaining 1 tablespoon of olive oil. Taste, and season with salt and black pepper. Add a sprinkle of red pepper flakes before serving.

Easy ingredient swaps: Dairy milk for the unsweetened plant milk / Kale, stemmed, or arugula for the spinach / Grated Parmesan cheese for the nutritional yeast

PENNE WITH ARTICHOKES, FETA & BLACK OLIVES

Penne with Artichokes, Feta and Black Olives

Prep to table: 20 minutes | Serves: 4 to 5

You've come to the right page if you want a tasty meal ready to roll out quickly. This combination of tender artichoke hearts and briny black olives offers a variety of tastes with "no two bites the same," according to one recipe tester. I usually make a big batch and eat it warm the first night, then serve the leftovers as a cold pasta salad. The feta cheese is not essential so skip it if you want to eat dairy-free. Another tester passed along a nice tip: When draining your pasta, use a silicone clip-on strainer so you don't have to remove it from the pot.

12 ounces penne or other short pasta

4 tablespoons olive oil

1 tablespoon red wine vinegar

2 tablespoons lemon juice

1 teaspoon dried oregano

¼ teaspoon red pepper flakes

½ teaspoon garlic powder

1 teaspoon salt

¾ cup pitted Kalamata black olives, halved

1 (14-ounce) can quartered artichoke hearts, drained

4 green onions, thinly sliced

1 pint (about 2 cups) cherry tomatoes, halved

10 to 12 large fresh basil leaves, cut into thin ribbons

¼ cup chopped fresh parsley (optional)

Freshly ground black pepper

Serving suggestion: ½ cup crumbled feta cheese / ½ cup toasted pine nuts

1. **Cook** the pasta in a large pot of salted water according to package directions. Drain, and return the pasta to the pot.

2. **Add** the olive oil, red wine vinegar, lemon juice, oregano, red pepper flakes, garlic, and salt and stir until mixed. Add the black olives, artichoke hearts, green onions, cherry tomatoes, basil, and parsley, if you have some on hand, and toss until combined. Taste and season with more salt and pepper, as needed.

3. **Serve** topped with a generous sprinkle of feta cheese and pine nuts.

Easy ingredient swaps: 2 medium garlic cloves, minced, for the garlic powder / Pitted black olives for the Kalamata olives / ½ red onion, thinly sliced, for the green onions

PESTO PASTA WITH SPINACH & CHERRY TOMATOES

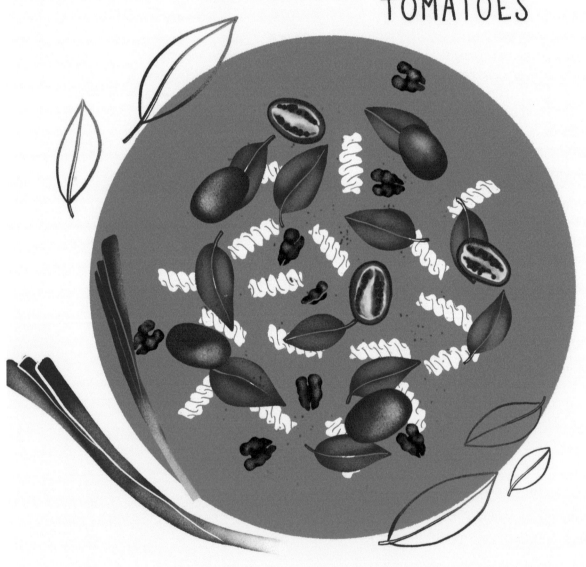

Pesto Pasta with Spinach and Cherry Tomatoes

Prep to table: 20 minutes | Serves 4 to 5

I couldn't decide between eating pasta and salad when crafting this recipe, so I split the difference. Pesto pasta is familiar, comforting, and a snap to throw together thanks to how easy it is to find the sauce. I like to mix it up by introducing vegetables and nuts that go well with basil pesto — in this case, spinach, cherry tomatoes, and walnuts. Bear in mind that the amount of salt and pepper you use will vary with the pesto you choose.

12 ounces short pasta, like penne or fusilli
½ teaspoon garlic powder
½ cup store bought basil pesto
3 generous handfuls fresh spinach
¾ cup halved cherry tomatoes

1 teaspoon salt
Freshly ground black pepper
¼ cup chopped fresh basil
½ cup walnut pieces

Serving suggestion: Small fresh mozzarella balls / 2 to 3 green onions, thinly sliced

1. **Cook** the pasta in salted water according to the package directions. Drain, reserving ¼ cup of the cooking water, and return the pasta to the pot.

2. **Stir** in the pesto, spinach, cherry tomatoes, and salt. Taste, and season with black pepper and more salt, if desired.

3. **Cover** the pot and let stand until the spinach is wilted.

4. **Add** the basil and walnuts and stir until combined. If the pasta becomes dry, or you want to reheat it, add some of the reserved cooking water or a little olive oil.

5. **Serve** topped with fresh mozzarella balls and green onions.

Easy ingredient swaps: Arugula for the spinach—about 2 cups if you don't want to overpower the rest of the dish since it's stronger tasting than spinach / Red bell pepper, chopped, for the cherry tomatoes / Toasted pine nuts for the walnuts / Parmesan cheese or nutritional yeast for the mozzarella balls

SESAME NOODLES

WITH EDAMAME AND PEANUTS

Sesame Noodles with Edamame and Peanuts

Prep to table: 15 minutes | Serves: 4

Bright red radishes, green edamame, and creamy avocado team up nicely here to create a stunning-looking dish. It also takes almost no time to prepare. But the best part is the way chewy soba noodles taste coated in tangy sesame dressing. Since soba noodle varieties vary, scan the package cooking instructions and adjust boiling time as needed. Note: This recipe calls for *toasted* sesame oil, which has a nutty flavor. Raw or *untoasted* sesame oil is lighter, more neutral in flavor, and a better cooking oil.

1 package (8- to 10-ounces) soba noodles

1 cup frozen peeled edamame

6 radishes, chopped

1 tablespoon toasted sesame oil

2 tablespoons rice wine vinegar

3 tablespoons soy sauce

1 cup chopped fresh mint

½ cup toasted sesame seeds

Salt

Freshly ground black pepper

Serving suggestion: 1 to 2 avocados, sliced / ¾ cup salted peanuts / 1 lime, cut into wedges

1. **Bring** a large pot of salted water to boil. Add the noodles and edamame and cook until both are done, about 3 to 4 minutes. Drain and rinse the noodles and edamame under cold water to prevent overcooking, and return them to the pot.

2. **Mix** in the radishes, sesame oil, rice wine vinegar, soy sauce, mint, and sesame seeds until well combined. Taste, and season with salt and black pepper.

3. **Serve** warm or cold, topped with avocado slices, peanuts, and lime wedges, for squeezing.

Easy ingredient swaps: Brown or white rice noodles, or spaghetti, for the soba noodles (follow the package cooking instructions) / Shredded carrots for the radishes / White wine vinegar for the rice wine vinegar / Chopped cilantro for the mint

sheet-pan
GNOCCHI WITH BRUSSELS SPROUTS

Sheet-Pan Gnocchi with Brussels Sprouts

Prep to table: 25 minutes | Serves: 3 to 4

Keeping a bag of frozen gnocchi on hand can be a dinnertime life saver. It's a standalone ingredient that needs only a stray veggie or two to taste like something special. For this recipe, I use cauliflower gnocchi but potato, sweet potato, kale, or whatever gnocchi works well, too. I often roast my gnocchi because I like the way they crisp up in an oven. Swap out the grated Parmesan for nutritional yeast, or omit it entirely — just add a bit more salt if you do. The lemon adds brightness. This is gourmet eating without the effort.

1 pound (3 to 4 cups) Brussels sprouts, halved

1 (12-ounce) bag frozen gnocchi

4 tablespoons olive oil, divided

½ teaspoon salt

½ teaspoon freshly ground black pepper

½ teaspoon red pepper flakes

2 teaspoons balsamic vinegar

Zest of 1 lemon

Serving suggestion: 2 tablespoons shaved or grated Parmesan / Chopped fresh basil / Lemon wedges or slices

1. **Preheat** the oven to 450 degrees. Line a sheet pan with parchment paper. Toss the Brussels sprouts and gnocchi on the sheet pan with the oil, salt, black pepper, red pepper flakes, and balsamic vinegar.

2. **Roast** long enough for the Brussels sprouts to be tender but bright green and for the gnocchi to brown lightly, about 20 minutes. Remove from the oven and transfer into a medium size bowl.

3. **Sprinkle** with lemon zest. Top with Parmesan and chopped basil, and serve with lemon slices for another hit of citrus flavor.

Easy ingredient swaps: Nutritional yeast for the grated Parmesan

CARROT SALAD
RIBBON with ALMONDS
& FRESH MINT

Carrot Ribbon Salad with Almonds and Fresh Mint

Prep to table: 20 minutes | Serves 4

I first made this recipe to impress Josiah, my then boyfriend and now husband. I'd planned a birthday picnic and wanted one of those moments where we're in the middle of nowhere (which often happens — we're hikers), I open my backpack, and we both see — *Wow! Carrot Ribbon Salad with Almonds and Fresh Mint!* He fell for it, and it's actually not much harder to make than peanut butter sandwiches. Okay, it's harder but worth it.

3 medium carrots
2 cups cooked quinoa
1 (15-ounce) can chickpeas, drained and rinsed
½ cup chopped roasted salted almonds
½ cup finely chopped fresh mint leaves

½ teaspoon salt
Freshly ground black pepper
2 to 3 cups fresh salad greens
Lemon Tahini Sauce (p. 146)

Serving suggestion: 1 lime, cut into wedges

1. **Trim** the tops of the carrots and use a vegetable peeler to peel all the way through the vegetable into a large mixing bowl.

2. **Stir** in the quinoa, chickpeas, almonds, mint, and salt until combined. Taste and add pepper and more salt, as needed.

3. **Toss** with fresh greens and dress with Lemon Tahini Sauce.

4. **Serve** with lime wedges.

Easy ingredient swaps: Couscous for the quinoa / White beans for the chickpeas / Chopped salted pistachios or cashews for the almonds / Store bought Green Goddess dressing or the creamy dressing of your choice for the Lemon Tahini Sauce / Lemon for the lime

KALE SALAD

WITH SUNFLOWER SEEDS &

lemon tahini dressing

Kale Salad with Sunflower Seeds and Lemon Tahini Dressing

Prep to table: 15 minutes | Serves: 2 to 3

I rarely order salads when I go out to eat. I find them a way to feel very full and then very hungry within 60 minutes — unless, that is, they're made with kale, far bulkier than salad greens. Kale can be tough and slightly bitter, so mellow it out by using your hands to work in the lemon juice and a fat, in this case tahini paste. For those who aren't convinced a salad is a real dinner, serve it with warm naan or avocado toast, or just toast.

½ cup Lemon Tahini Sauce (p. 146),
    plus more if needed
1 bunch (2 to 3 cups) kale, stemmed
    and chopped
4 green onions, thinly sliced
4 to 6 radishes, thinly sliced

2 cups cooked corn
2 medium carrots, peeled and sliced
1 cup cooked brown rice
½ cup roasted sunflower seeds
Salt
Freshly ground black pepper

Serving suggestion: Toast

1. **Pour** the Lemon Tahini Sauce into a large salad bowl. Add the kale and massage the dressing into the leaves to soften.

2. **Add** the green onions, radishes, corn, rice, and sunflower seeds and toss until combined. Add more dressing, if you'd like. Taste, and season with salt and black pepper.

3. **Serve** with toast.

Easy ingredient swaps: Store bought Green Goddess Dressing, or your own creamy blend, for the Lemon Tahini Sauce / Farro for the brown rice / Walnut pieces for the sunflower seeds

ROASTED BEET & RADISH SALAD with GOAT CHEESE

Roasted Beet and Radish Salad with Goat Cheese

Prep to table: 50 minutes | Serves 3 to 4

My mom is an artist. She tends to fill her grocery cart with fruit and vegetables chosen largely for their beauty, which helps explain why I appreciate beets and radishes. This salad, featuring both, is the kind of extravagantly bright meal my mother would love. I didn't catch on to the practice of roasting radishes until a few years ago. Roasting turns a radish into a different vegetable — one that's mild and creamy instead of sharp and tangy, more root vegetable than salad fixing. I'm a fan. Small tip: Peel your beets after roasting them; the skin just slips off.

4 to 5 medium red beets, cut into wedges
4 tablespoons olive oil, divided
¾ teaspoon salt, plus more to taste
1 teaspoon dried thyme
1 cup trimmed and halved radishes
Freshly ground black pepper

4 to 5 cups mild salad greens
2 green onions, thinly sliced
½ cup crumbled goat cheese
½ to ¾ cup walnut pieces
Simple Salad Dressing (p. 147)

1. **Preheat** the oven to 375 degrees. Toss the beets on a sheet pan with 2 tablespoons olive oil, ½ teaspoon salt, and the thyme, and roast for 25 minutes.

2. **Remove** the pan from the oven and raise the oven temperature to 425 degrees. Add the radishes, the remaining 2 tablespoons of olive oil and ¼ teaspoon of salt, and toss with the beets. Return the pan to the oven and roast for another 15 minutes, or until the beets are tender when pierced with a fork.

3. **Peel** the beets once they've cooled. Combine the peeled beets and radishes in a medium salad bowl with the greens, green onions, goat cheese, and walnuts. Just before serving, dress with Simple Salad Dressing, and toss.

Easy ingredient swaps: Feta or Iberico for the goat cheese / Roasted pistachios or almond slivers for the walnuts / Vinegar and oil salad dressing of your choice for the Simple Salad Dressing

SALAD LYONNAISE *without* THE BACON

Salade Lyonnaise without the Bacon

Prep to table: 30 minutes | Serves: 3 to 4

Salade Lyonnaise, a popular offering in French bistros, is adored by fans of runny eggs and bacon. Here, I've swapped out the meat for portobello mushrooms and kept the eggs. To make the mushrooms sing, I cut them thick and sear, browning them on both sides so they're crisp outside and soft inside. (Fun fact: Portobello mushrooms are the mature version of cremini mushrooms.) I'm among those who love this dish served with an egg on top, the yolk blending in with the oil and vinegar dressing. In keeping with the one-pot theme, this recipe calls for fried eggs, but poaching is more typical.

2 to 3 tablespoons oil, divided, plus
   more if needed
4 to 5 medium-large portobello mushrooms,
   thickly sliced
Salt
Freshly ground black pepper
1/3 pound thin green beans, or haricot
   verts, trimmed

8 garlic cloves, quartered
1 teaspoon dried thyme
1 cup walnut pieces
1 medium red onion, thinly sliced
4 cups chicory lettuce or salad greens
Simple Salad Dressing (p. 147)

Serving suggestion: 3 to 4 fried eggs

1. **Heat** 1 tablespoon of oil in a large skillet over high heat. Add the mushrooms in batches—you want each slice to touch the pan. Sauté them on high heat, lightly browning both sides. If the mushrooms get dry, add more oil. Season with salt and pepper as you cook. Transfer the cooked mushrooms to a paper towel.

2. **Add** 1 tablespoon of oil to the same skillet, and heat. Add the green beans, garlic, and thyme and sauté until the beans are just tender and bright green, about 4 minutes. Stir in the walnuts and cook for 1 minute.

3. **Remove** from the heat. Stir in the mushrooms and red onion.

4. **Fill** a salad bowl with chicory lettuce or salad greens and lightly dress with the Simple Salad Dressing. Add the mixture from the skillet and toss. Divide the tossed salad into 4 shallow bowls or plates.

5. **Fry** the eggs in the same skillet—I like them sunnyside up. Add more oil if needed. Season with salt and black pepper, and serve one egg on top of each salad.

Easy ingredient swaps: Cremini mushrooms for the portobellos / Frozen green beans for the fresh green beans / Lemon juice, white wine vinegar, or the vinaigrette of your choice for the Simple Salad Dressing

WARM POTATO & BAKED CAULIFLOWER

— SALAD WITH WALNUTS

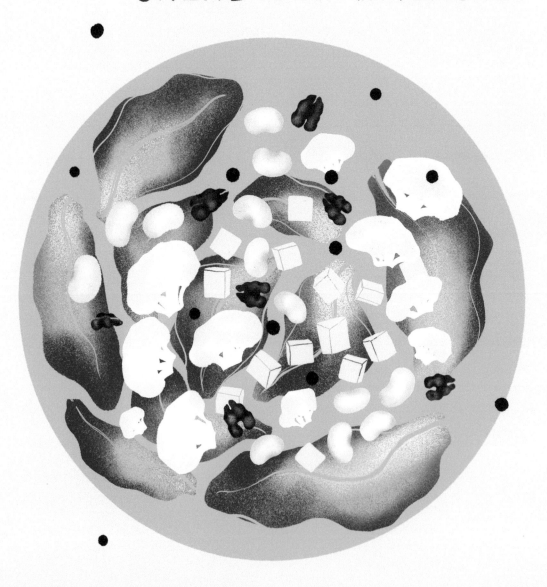

Warm Potato and Baked Cauliflower Salad with Walnuts

Prep to table: 50 minutes | Serves: 4

The idea here is potato salad but healthier, thanks to the addition of cauliflower and beans. I roast the vegetables with lots of garlic and add capers to give them a salty boost. My potato of choice is the Yukon Gold, but just about any thin-skinned potato will do. Serve this salad warm, or bring it with you on your next picnic, with or without the salad greens.

2 medium Yukon Gold potatoes, cut into
   1-inch chunks
1 medium cauliflower, chopped
1 (15-ounce) can white beans, drained and rinsed
¼ cup olive oil
8 garlic cloves, chopped

½ teaspoon salt, plus more to taste
¼ cup pesto
½ cup walnut pieces
3 tablespoons capers
Freshly ground black pepper

Serving suggestion: 4 cups mild salad greens / Simple Salad Dressing (p. 147)

1. **Preheat** the oven to 400 degrees. Line a large sheet pan with parchment paper. Add the potatoes, cauliflower, beans, olive oil, garlic, and salt and toss until coated.

2. **Spread** the vegetables on the pan and bake for 15 minutes. Remove from the oven, flip the vegetables, and return to the oven to bake for another 25 minutes, or until the potatoes are soft.

3. **Transfer** the cooked vegetables to a large serving bowl. Add the pesto, walnuts, capers, and black pepper and toss until combined.

4. **Serve** the potato salad as is, or tossed with salad greens and Simple Salad Dressing.

Easy ingredient swaps: Chickpeas for the white beans / White wine vinegar or lemon juice for the Simple Salad Dressing

CAULIFLOWER & SWEET POTATO BOWL WITH tangy MOJO SAUCE

Cauliflower and Sweet Potato Bowl with Tangy Mojo Sauce

Prep to table: 40 minutes | Serves: 4

My brother didn't have an oven for years. When I visited his tiny apartment in Paris for dinner, I learned something new. You mean you don't have to roast sweet potatoes in an oven to enjoy them? Nope. They soften right up with just a few minutes of sautéing. The key is to cover the skillet and create a tiny steam room, softening the center of sweet potato chunks while the edges sear. (I like mine unpeeled, but up to you!) Another fairly recent, though unrelated, discovery: cauliflower rice. It packs more vitamins, minerals, and phytonutrients than rice, and weighs in at one-eighth the calories. It's also very mild. I replace rice with it every chance it makes sense.

4 tablespoons olive oil, divided
1 medium sweet potato, chopped
1 teaspoon salt, divided, plus more to taste
Freshly ground black pepper
3 garlic cloves, minced

1 (14-ounce) package frozen cauliflower rice
1 yellow onion, thinly sliced
1 (15-ounce) can black beans, drained and rinsed
½ cup chopped fresh parsley

Serving suggestion: 1 avocado, sliced / ½ cup pico de gallo or salsa fresca / Orange and Lime Mojo Sauce (p. 147) / Toasted pumpkin seeds

1. **Heat** 2 tablespoons of olive oil in a large skillet over medium heat. Add the potatoes and season with ½ teaspoon salt and some black pepper. Cover the pan and cook for 3 minutes.

2. **Remove** the lid and cook until the potatoes turn golden brown, about 3 to 5 minutes. Flip them, and cook until tender, another 3 to 5 minutes. Transfer to a paper towel.

3. **Heat** the remaining 2 tablespoons of olive oil in the same skillet, over medium heat. Add the garlic and onion and cook until the onion softens, about 3 to 4 minutes. Add the cauliflower rice, season with the remaining ½ teaspoon of salt, and sauté until cooked through, 4 to 6 minutes.

4. **Stir** in the black beans and parsley and cook until warmed, about 1 minute. Season with black pepper and more salt, to taste.

5. **Spoon** the steaming cauliflower rice and black bean mixture into bowls. Top with the sweet potatoes, sliced avocado, and pico de gallo. Dress with the Orange and Lime Mojo Sauce and serve with a sprinkle of toasted pumpkin seeds.

Easy ingredient swaps: Pinto beans for the black beans / Any salsa for the pico de gallo / Squirt of fresh orange and lemon or lime for the Orange and Lime Mojo Sauce

KALE & TOMATO SHAKSHUKA with feta

Kale and Tomato Shakshuka with Feta

Prep to table: 45 minutes I Serves: 4

Shakshuka is said to have originated in mid-16th century North Africa shortly after tomatoes were introduced. Today, it's mostly served as a brunch dish but can also make for a satisfying dinner. With shakshuka, you are basically poaching eggs and reducing tomatoes at the same time. I build in flavor and texture by adding hearty greens. To successfully bake the eggs, you need a skillet with a lid. If you find yourself without a lid, tin foil will do. I serve this dish with thick toast for dipping and devouring.

3 tablespoons olive oil
1 medium yellow onion, thinly sliced
1 large bunch kale, stemmed, chopped
4 garlic cloves, minced
2 teaspoons ground cumin
2 teaspoons paprika

1 (28-ounce) can diced tomatoes, with juices
1 teaspoon salt
Freshly ground black pepper
4 eggs
½ cup crumbled goat cheese

Serving suggestion: Hot sauce / Avocado, sliced / Toast

1. **Heat** the olive oil in a large skillet over medium heat. Add the onion and sauté until soft, about 3 to 4 minutes. Add the kale leaves in batches, adding more as they wilt, and cook for 4 more minutes. Add the garlic, cumin, and paprika and sauté for 1 more minute.

2. **Stir** in the tomatoes, salt and black pepper, and cook gently for 10 minutes.

3. **Make** 4 divots in the tomato kale mixture with the back of a large spoon. Crack an egg into each divot, and sprinkle everything with goat cheese.

4. **Cover** and continue cooking over medium heat until the eggs are just set, about 15 minutes. Taste, and add more salt and pepper, if needed.

5. **Scoop** the mixture into bowls, making sure each serving gets an egg. Add hot sauce, sliced avocado, and a side of crusty toasted bread.

Easy ingredient swaps: Spinach for the kale / Feta or some other salty cheese for the goat cheese

SAUTÉED BEANS
& greens with LEMON ZEST

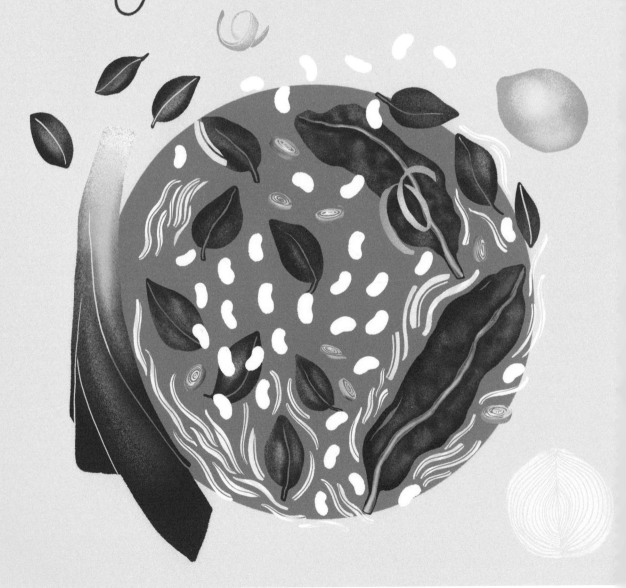

Sautéed Beans and Greens with Lemon Zest

Prep to table: 25 minutes | Serves: 3 to 4

I often rely on beans to make meat-free dishes more substantial and protein-rich. They tend to play a supporting role and only occasionally show up in recipe names. But here they're a key ingredient — and why shouldn't they be? Beans absorb flavors beautifully and add a creamy richness to many meals. I recommend eating this bean-hearty dish, which is more stew than soup, with thick slices of crusty bread so you can sop up all the flavors.

¼ cup olive oil

2 leeks, thinly sliced

2 teaspoons dried rosemary

8 garlic cloves, chopped

½ teaspoon salt, plus more to taste

¼ teaspoon red pepper flakes

4 cups chopped spinach or kale, or both

1 (15-ounce) can cannellini beans, drained and rinsed

1½ cups vegetable broth

¼ teaspoon freshly ground black pepper, plus more to taste

Zest and juice of 1 lemon

¼ cup grated Romano or Parmesan cheese

Serving suggestion: Thick slices crusty bread, toasted

1. **Heat** the olive oil in a large sauté pan or skillet over medium heat. Add the leeks and rosemary and cook, stirring often, until soft, 4 to 6 minutes. Add the garlic, salt, and red pepper flakes and cook for 1 minute.

2. **Add** the greens in handfuls, cooking and stirring until the leaves wilt.

3. **Add** the cannellini beans, broth, and black pepper, and stir until combined. Bring to a boil, and then lower the heat and simmer until the liquid thickens, 6 to 8 minutes.

4. **Remove** from heat and stir in the lemon juice, lemon zest, and Romano cheese. Taste and add more salt and black pepper, if you'd like.

5. **Serve** with slices of toasted bread.

Easy ingredient swap: 2 medium yellow onions, chopped, for the leeks / Any white beans for the cannellini beans / Water for the broth / Nutritional yeast for the grated cheese

STOVE TOP *vegetable* FRITTATA

Stove Top Vegetable Frittata

Prep to table: 15 minutes I Serves: 2

When I'm tired and have zero interest in cooking, I often make myself a frittata. Traditionally thick, custardy, and baked in an oven, this stove-top version is simpler and thinner. Pick just about any vegetable combination you like for the filling. I tend to be guided by whatever's in my fridge but visit the recipe-free cooking section (p. 141) if you want inspiration. Among my favorite combinations: mushrooms and spinach, tomatoes and broccoli, and kale and cooked potatoes. Pick any cheese you like, shred it, and add it about halfway through the cooking process so it melts into the eggs. All that's left to do is to make yourself a side salad.

2 tablespoons olive oil
1 medium onion, chopped
½ teaspoon salt, divided, plus more to taste
2 to 3 cups vegetables, chopped

Freshly ground black pepper
4 eggs, beaten
½ cup shredded Gruyere cheese

Serving suggestion: Fresh parsley, chopped / Chunky salsa

1. **Heat** the olive oil over medium heat in a 9-inch skillet with a lid. Add the onion and cook with a sprinkle of salt until it softens, about 3 to 4 minutes.

2. **Add** the chopped vegetables of your choice. Sauté with ¼ teaspoon salt and black pepper until almost cooked—how long depends on the vegetables you use.

3. **Whisk** together the eggs, ¼ teaspoon salt, and black pepper in a small bowl. Pour the eggs over the vegetables and stir until evenly blended. Let the eggs cook until they start to set.

4. **Add** the cheese. Loosen the edges of the frittata with a knife or spatula and tilt the pan so the eggy mix doesn't pool. Cover the skillet with the lid and keep the heat low until the eggs are cooked through, about 4 to 5 minutes.

5. **Cut** into wedges and serve topped with chopped parsley and a side of salsa.

Easy ingredient swaps: Cheese of your choice for the Gruyere

BLACK-EYED PEA SOUP
with SPINACH & TOMATOES

Black-Eyed Pea Soup with Spinach and Tomatoes

Prep to table: 35 minutes | Serves: 4

My mom insisted we eat black-eyed peas on New Year's day for good luck. I consider myself lucky and also believe in hedging my bets, so pass the black-eyed peas. Stirring the spinach, onion, and oil together with some flour mimics a roux, and serves as a thickening agent for this hearty soup. Add more broth if you want it soupier, and fire-roasted diced tomatoes if you like your soup with some heat. This is the best way to eat black-eyed peas that I've found. Happy new year.

1 (12- to 16-ounce) bag frozen spinach
1 large yellow onion, chopped
5 tablespoons olive oil
¼ cup all-purpose flour
1 red bell pepper, seeded, chopped
8 garlic cloves, chopped
1 tablespoon dried oregano
1 tablespoon dried thyme
1 tablespoon dried basil

1 teaspoon paprika
1 teaspoon salt, plus more if needed
1 teaspoon freshly ground black pepper
3 ¼ cups vegetable broth, divided, plus
  more as needed
1 (24-ounce) can diced tomatoes, with juices
1 cup frozen corn
1 (16-ounce) can black-eyed peas, drained
  and rinsed

Serving suggestion: Feta cheese / Cornbread

1. **Sauté** the spinach, onion, and oil in a large pot over medium heat until the onion begins to soften, 3 to 4 minutes. Remove from the heat and stir in the flour until the spinach and onion are evenly coated.

2. **Return** the pot to the stove and add the bell pepper, garlic, oregano, thyme, basil, paprika, salt, and black pepper. Sauté about 3 minutes. Dribble in about ¼ cup of vegetable broth and stir to prevent the ingredients from drying out.

3. **Add** the remaining 3 cups of broth, tomatoes, corn, and black-eyed peas and bring to a boil over medium-high heat. Lower the heat and simmer, stirring often, until the soup has thickened and the peppers have softened but still have some snap, about 15 minutes.

4. **Taste** and season with additional salt and pepper, if needed. Top with a sprinkling of feta cheese. Serve with cornbread.

Easy ingredient swaps: White northern beans or black beans for the black-eyed peas.

BUTTERNUT SQUASH
& SHIITAKE SOUP
MUSHROOM

Butternut Squash and Shiitake Mushroom Soup

Prep to table: 45 minutes | Serves: 4

Shiitake mushrooms are rich in *umami*, which is Japanese for savory, one of the five basic tastes (sweet, sour, salty, and bitter are the others). Teaming them up with a classic butternut squash soup makes it heartier, with more texture and taste. The easiest way to make this golden soup is to buy already-peeled and chopped squash, which you can generally find frozen and in the produce aisle. Eat this soup chunky, with the mushrooms floating in the soup, or smooth.

1 medium onion, chopped
¼ cup olive oil, plus more for drizzling
6 medium-large shiitake mushrooms, thinly sliced
½ teaspoon salt, plus more to taste

½ teaspoon freshly ground black pepper, plus more to taste
4 garlic garlic cloves, minced
2 cups cubed butternut squash
3 cups vegetable broth, plus more if needed

Serving suggestion: Olive oil / Toasted pumpkin seeds

1. **Sauté** the onion and olive oil in a large soup pot over medium heat until soft and fragrant, about 3 to 4 minutes. Add the mushrooms, season with salt and pepper, and continue to sauté until the mushrooms soften, about 5 minutes. Add the garlic and sauté for 1 minute.

2. **Add** the butternut squash and sauté for 4 more minutes. Pour in the broth and bring the mixture to boil over medium-high heat. Lower the heat and simmer, with the lid partially on, until the squash is very soft and naturally breaking down, 25 to 30 minutes.

3. **Blend** the soup using a hand-held immersion blender until you get the consistency you want. Add more broth if you'd like it soupier. Season with salt and black pepper.

4. **Serve** drizzled with a little olive oil and topped with pumpkin seeds.

Easy ingredient swaps: Any small mushrooms for the shiitake mushrooms / Roasted slivered almonds for the pumpkin seeds

CABBAGE & WHITE BEAN SOUP WITH HERBS DE PROVENCE

Cabbage and White Bean Soup with Herbes de Provence

Prep to table: 35 minutes | Serves: 4 to 6

Everybody has a rainy day meal — the kind that's comforting in part because it's so familiar. This one is mine, and it can be yours, too. The herbs de Provence, onions, fennel, and garlic fill up my kitchen with good smells. It's delicious and nourishing. Toss in any number of different vegetables, including carrots, celery, fennel bulb, mushrooms, and spinach. Just cut them into bite size pieces and add with the potatoes during the boil phase. The sun will come out.

2 tablespoons olive oil

1 yellow onion, chopped

6 garlic cloves, minced

5 cups vegetable broth

2 large or 3 small Yukon Gold potatoes, cut into 1-inch chunks

½ head red or green cabbage, sliced, roughly chopped

1 (15-ounce) can cannellini beans, drained and rinsed

1 ½ tablespoons herbs de Provence

1 teaspoon fennel seeds

2 teaspoons salt, plus more if needed

Freshly ground black pepper

Serving suggestion: Olive oil / Shaved Parmesan / Fresh basil, thinly sliced

1. **Heat** the olive oil in a large soup pot over low heat. Add the onion and sauté until it softens and becomes fragrant, about 3 to 4 minutes. Add the garlic and sauté for another minute.

2. **Add** the vegetable broth, potatoes, cabbage, beans, herbes de Provence, fennel seeds, and salt and bring to a boil.

3. **Simmer**, covered, until the potatoes are tender, about 25 minutes.

4. **Season** with black pepper and blend with a handheld immersion blender for a slighter smoother and thicker soup, if you'd like.

5. **Ladle** the soup into large bowls. Top with a drizzle of olive oil, a sprinkle of Parmesan ribbons, and chopped fresh basil.

Easy ingredient swaps: Water for the broth / Cooked navy beans or any white bean for the cannellini beans / Caraway seeds for the fennel seeds

CAULIFLOWER &
chile CHILI

Cauliflower and Chile Chili

Prep to table: 45 minutes | Serves: 5 to 6

This soup is inspired by creamy white chili, or chili based on green chiles instead of the more common red chiles. Our recipe testing crew loved it, and suggested additional ways to rev up the heat factor, like adding pickled serrano chiles. When choosing jalapeños, it's worth knowing that the older they are, the spicier; the beauties with smooth skin tend to be milder. A little maple syrup gives this dish the sweetness that keeps it in chili land rather than sliding into plain old white bean soup. Make it a day ahead; it's more flavorful when the ingredients spend more time together.

2 tablespoons olive oil

1 yellow onion, chopped

1 red bell pepper, seeded, chopped

1 jalapeño pepper, seeded, finely chopped

5 garlic cloves, minced

1 ½ teaspoons chili powder

1 teaspoon ground coriander

1 teaspoon dried oregano

2 teaspoons salt

6 cups vegetable broth

1 medium cauliflower, chopped

1 medium Yukon Gold potato, chopped

2 (15-ounce) cans pinto beans, drained
  and rinsed

1 (7-ounce) can fire-roasted green chiles

2 teaspoons maple syrup

Juice of 1 lime

Freshly ground black pepper

Serving suggestion: Chopped fresh cilantro / Fresh radishes, thinly sliced / Serrano peppers, pickled / Shredded cheese / Cornbread

1. **Sauté** the oil, onion, red bell pepper, and jalapeño pepper in a large soup pot over low heat until the onion is soft, about 3 to 4 minutes. Add the garlic, chili powder, coriander, oregano, and salt and continue to sauté for 2 minutes.

2. **Add** the vegetable broth, cauliflower, potatoes, pinto beans, green chiles, and maple syrup and bring to boil over medium-high heat. Decrease the heat to medium-low and simmer until the cauliflower is soft, 20 to 25 minutes.

3. **Stir** in the lime juice and season with additional salt and back pepper.

4. **Top** with chopped cilantro, radishes, pickled serrano peppers, or the shredded cheese of your choice. Serve with cornbread on the side.

Easy ingredient swaps: Any thin-skinned potato for the Yukon Gold / Brown sugar for the maple syrup

creamy PEA & CAULIFLOWER SOUP

Creamy Pea and Cauliflower Soup

Prep to table: 40 minutes | Serves: 5 to 8

I live in San Francisco, a mostly temperate climate, which means I frequently find myself startled by the arrival of the holidays or envious of photos of friends wearing flip-flops. One blustery cold day in August, I created this recipe to warm me up, while still celebrating the fresh taste of summer. Here, mild-flavored cauliflower makes a nice base for the brightness of green peas, tangy lemon, and fresh chives. This soup takes on a whole new identity when served cold — it's like vichyssoise. I recommend keeping the soup unblended and warm on cold days, and smooth and cool on hot days.

2 tablespoons olive oil, plus more for drizzling
1 medium yellow onion, chopped
1 large cauliflower, chopped
2 garlic cloves, minced
1 teaspoon caraway seeds (optional)
6 cups vegetable broth (less for a
  smaller cauliflower)

1 teaspoon salt
6 cups frozen peas
1 teaspoon lemon juice
3 tablespoons nutritional yeast
2 teaspoons soy sauce
Freshly ground black pepper

Serving suggestion: Olive oil / ¼ cup finely chopped fresh chives / ½ cup chopped roasted hazelnuts

1. **Sauté** the olive oil, onion, and cauliflower in a large soup pot over medium heat for 6 minutes. Add the garlic and caraway seeds, if you want more bite, and sauté for 2 more minutes.

2. **Add** the vegetable broth and salt and bring to a boil over medium-high heat. Decrease the heat and simmer for 15 minutes.

3. **Mix** in the frozen peas and simmer for 7 more minutes. Remove from the heat. If you want to blend the ingredients, this is a good time to do so.

4. **Stir** in the lemon juice, nutritional yeast, and soy sauce. Taste, and add salt and black pepper, as needed.

5. **Top** with a drizzle of olive oil and the chopped chives and nuts.

Easy ingredient swaps: Grated Parmesan cheese for the nutritional yeast / Tamari for the soy sauce (for a gluten-free soup) / Chopped green onions for the chives / Any roasted nuts for the hazelnuts

FIRE-ROASTED TOMATO TORTILLA SOUP

Fire-Roasted Tomato Tortilla Soup

Prep to table: 30 minutes | Serves: 5 to 6

I like to make this soup when entertaining a group of friends with unknown food preferences. Tortilla soup is familiar, well-liked, and easy to customize thanks to a multitude of topping options — kind of like a taco bar for soup. I've discovered most people like it spicy, which explains the chili powder, fire-roasted tomatoes, and chipotle peppers in adobo sauce (add two of the peppers if you like it extra spicy). Chipotle peppers in adobo sauce can generally be found in the Latin food section of the grocery store. If you can't find them, a spicy salsa will do. I like my soup with beans but skip them, if you'd rather. Just before serving, crumble tortilla chips in the soup, and spoon it all up.

2 tablespoons olive oil

1 medium yellow onion, chopped

2 garlic cloves, minced

1 tablespoon chili powder

2 teaspoons salt

4 cups vegetable broth, plus more as needed

2 cups frozen corn

1 (15-ounce) can pinto beans, drained and rinsed (optional)

1 can (28-ounce) crushed fire-roasted tomatoes

1 to 2 chipotle peppers in adobo sauce, chopped finely

3 cups crumbled tortilla chips

Freshly ground black pepper

Serving suggestion: Fresh cilantro, chopped / Green cabbage, sliced, roughly chopped / 1 or 2 avocados, sliced / Tortilla chips

1. **Sauté** the oil and onion in a large soup pot over low heat until the onion is soft, about 3 to 4 minutes. Add the garlic, chili powder, and salt and continue to sauté for 2 minutes.

2. **Add** the vegetable broth, corn, and pinto beans, if you'd like a thicker soup, along with the tomatoes, and chipotle peppers in adobo sauce and bring to a boil. Lower the heat and simmer about 15 minutes. Add more broth if you'd like a soupier consistency.

3. **Stir** in the tortilla chips and season with additional salt and back pepper, to taste. Let stand for 2 minutes.

4. **Serve** with bowls of cilantro, chopped cabbage, avocado, and extra tortilla chips.

Easy ingredient swaps: Black beans for the pinto beans / ½ cup spicy chunky salsa for the chipotles in adobo sauce

hearty MOROCCAN VEGETABLE STEW

Hearty Moroccan Vegetable Stew

Prep to table: 40 minutes | Serves: 4

This dish borrows its flavor profile from Moroccan harira, a flavorful stew traditionally made with chickpeas, fava beans, and lamb. In the plant-based version, the flavor and texture draws from chickpeas, butternut squash, and other vegetables cooked in Middle Eastern spices. This version resembles a stew; add more broth if you want it soupier.

4 tablespoons olive oil

1 large yellow onion, chopped

2 medium carrots, peeled and sliced

1 large zucchini, cut into 1-inch slices

5 to 7 garlic cloves, minced

½ teaspoon red pepper flakes

1 teaspoon ground turmeric

1 teaspoon ground cumin

1 teaspoon salt, plus more to taste

1 teaspoon freshly ground black pepper,
   plus more to taste

4 cups vegetable broth, plus more as needed

1 cup cubed butternut squash

1 (15-ounce) can crushed tomatoes, with juice

1 (15-ounce) can chickpeas, drained and rinsed

2 to 3 cups fresh spinach or arugula

Zest of 1 lemon

½ cup chopped roasted almonds

Serving suggestion: Chopped parsley / Toasted pita bread

1. **Sauté** the olive oil, onion, carrots, and zucchini in a large soup pot over medium heat for 5 minutes. Add the garlic and continue to sauté until fragrant, about a minute.

2. **Stir** in the red pepper flakes, turmeric, cumin, salt, and black pepper. Add the vegetable broth, butternut squash, crushed tomatoes, and chickpeas and bring to a boil over medium heat. Decrease the heat and simmer until the squash is tender, about 30 minutes. Add more broth if you'd like it soupier.

3. **Stir** in the spinach, lemon zest, and almonds. Taste, add salt and black pepper as needed. Top with parsley and serve with toasted pita bread.

Easy ingredient swaps: 3 stalks celery, chopped, for the zucchini / 1 cup chopped sweet potatoes or new potatoes, for the butternut squash / 1 tablespoon lemon juice for the lemon zest

JOSIAH'S *sweet potato* CHILI

Josiah's Sweet Potato Chili

Prep to table: 40 minutes | Serves: 6 to 8

When 2020 kicked into full-on pandemic mode and we all stocked up on beans, my husband Josiah seized the moment. This high-protein sweet potato chili started out as a simple bean and tomato soup, but with each new round he tweaked it just a bit. Finally he landed on a recipe that marries the beans and tomatoes with chili spices and sweet potatoes — comfort food jam-packed with fiber and vitamins. It's a mainstay of our diet to this day. This recipe makes enough for a crowd of six to eight, so adjust quantities as needed.

1 tablespoon olive oil

1 medium sweet onion, chopped

2 garlic cloves, minced

1 tablespoon chili powder

2 teaspoons ground cumin

1 tablespoon dried oregano

1 teaspoon smoked paprika

1 teaspoon salt, plus more to taste

1 (24-ounce) can fire-roasted tomatoes

3 cups vegetable broth

2 medium sweet potatoes, peeled, cubed

1 cup dried lentils, rinsed

1 (16-ounce) can black beans, drained and rinsed

1 tablespoon maple syrup

1 (16-ounce) container red salsa

Freshly ground black pepper

Serving suggestion: Thinly sliced red onion or green onions / Grated cheddar cheese / 2 avocados, sliced / Tortilla chips

1. **Heat** the olive oil in a large soup pot over medium heat. Add the onion and sauté for 4 minutes. Add the garlic, chili powder, cumin, oregano, paprika, and salt and sauté for 1 more minute.

2. **Stir** in 3 cups of water, tomatoes, vegetable broth, sweet potatoes, lentils, black beans, maple syrup, and salsa and bring to a boil over medium-high heat. Decrease the heat and simmer, stirring occasionally, for 30 minutes.

3. **Taste**, and season with salt and black pepper. Spoon into bowls and serve with the toppings of your choice.

Easy ingredient swaps: Paprika or cayenne pepper for the smoked paprika / Butternut squash for the sweet potato

MISO SOUP *with* SHIITAKE MUSHROOMS

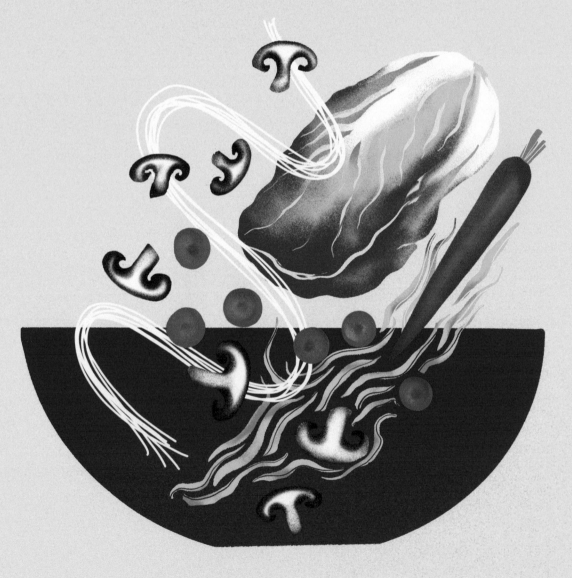

Miso Soup with Shiitake Mushrooms

Prep to table: 20 minutes | Serves: 3 to 4

I started experimenting with miso paste after trying, and failing, to find a packaged miso soup that I like. Miso, a savory Japanese paste produced by fermenting soybeans with the fungus *aspergillus orzae*, is known for its strong umami flavor. Miso is a complete source of protein and rich in vitamins and minerals — if you don't boil the living daylights out of it. So I suggest turning off the heat before adding it to your soup. For the other ingredients, go with green cabbage, if you can; the red turns the soup a little murky, though it will still taste great. For the rice noodles, choose thin ones that need up to four minutes of cooking time so you don't overcook your vegetables. They don't deserve it.

5 garlic cloves, minced

1 tablespoon light, untoasted sesame oil

½ pound shiitake mushrooms, sliced

2 large carrots, thinly sliced

6 tablespoons soy sauce

½ cup cubed firm tofu

5½ cups water

8 ounces thin rice noodles

½ head small green cabbage, sliced, roughly chopped

3 green onions, thinly sliced, divided

2 tablespoons dried seaweed (optional)

¼ cup miso paste (white, yellow, or red)

Serving suggestion: Chopped parsley / Soy sauce / Red pepper flakes

1. **Sauté** the garlic and sesame oil in a soup pot over medium heat for about 2 minutes. Add the mushrooms and cook until fragrant, about 3 minutes. Stir in the carrots, soy sauce, and tofu and cook for 1 more minute to lock in the flavors.

2. **Add** the water and bring to a boil. Lower the heat and simmer until the vegetables have softened, about 5 minutes. Stir in the noodles, cabbage, and half the green onions. Simmer until the noodles have softened, 2 to 4 minutes. Turn off the heat and stir in the seaweed, if you want more salty flavor, and miso paste.

3. **Serve** in bowls topped with the remaining green onions and parsley. Include extra soy sauce and red pepper flakes so you can turn up the intensity, if you want.

Easy ingredient swaps: Olive oil for the sesame oil / Chopped fresh spinach for the cabbage / 1 leek, thinly sliced, for the green onions / 1-inch piece (1 tablespoon) fresh ginger, grated, for the red pepper flakes

persian-inspired
BEANS & GREENS
SOUP

Persian-Inspired Beans and Greens Soup

Prep to table: 35 minutes | Serves: 4 to 6

This soup was lightly inspired by ash reshteh, a Persian soup made with white beans, greens, and noodles. The original is delicious but making it can be a production. So I've cut out a couple of steps, like chilling the beans and herbs a day ahead of time. I also removed the pasta to make it more soup than stew. The result is a hearty but not heavy, easy-to-assemble dinner. Top it off with a dollop of cooling yogurt and freshly chopped chives.

3 tablespoons olive oil

1 medium yellow onion, finely chopped

4 garlic cloves

½ teaspoon ground turmeric

1 teaspoon salt, plus more to taste

1 can (15-ounce) any white bean, drained and rinsed

1 cup dried lentils, rinsed

1 teaspoon dried dill

6 cups vegetable broth

1 bunch fresh cilantro, chopped

4 cups chopped fresh spinach

¼ teaspoon cayenne pepper

Serving suggestion: Chopped fresh chives / Chopped roasted hazelnuts / Plain Greek yogurt

1. **Sauté** the olive oil and onion in a large soup pot over medium heat until the onion is fragrant and soft, about 3 to 4 minutes. Add the garlic, turmeric, and salt and sauté for 1 more minute.

2. **Stir** in the white beans, lentils, dill, and vegetable broth, making sure nothing gets stuck to the bottom of the pot, and bring to a boil. Reduce the heat and simmer for 10 minutes.

3. **Add** the cilantro, spinach, and cayenne pepper and simmer for 10 to 15 minutes. Season with salt and black pepper, to taste.

4. **Serve** with a sprinkling of fresh chives and chopped hazelnuts, and a generous dollop of plain yogurt.

Easy ingredient swap: Swiss chard, arugula, collard greens, or kale for the spinach / Any roasted nuts for the hazelnuts

RED BEET & WHITE BEAN BORSCHT with CARAWAY SEEDS

Red Beet and White Bean Borscht with Caraway Seeds

Prep to table: 45 minutes | Serves: 4

This soup gets its tang from pickle juice, a secret passed along to me by a Ukrainian friend who grew up making borscht. I think it adds something special but the soup tastes perfectly good without it. When prepping the beets, make it easier on yourself by just focusing on the gritty bits — it doesn't have to be perfectly skinned. Wear an apron or shirt you don't care about; you want to avoid getting beet juice on anything that's not already pink. If your beets come with greens, chop them up and add to the soup in Step 3. I use cannellini beans for this dish but just about any white bean will do.

½ teaspoon caraway seeds

3 tablespoons olive oil

1 medium yellow onion, chopped

½ small red cabbage, sliced, roughly chopped

2 carrots, peeled, thinly sliced

2 medium beets, peeled, chopped

1 medium Yukon Gold potato, chopped

1 ½ teaspoon salt, plus more to taste

4 cups vegetable broth, plus more as needed

1 (15-ounce) can white beans, drained
  and rinsed

2 teaspoons dried dill

2 tablespoons unsweetened pickle juice

Freshly ground black pepper

Serving suggestion: Avocado, sliced / Fresh dill, chopped

1. **Heat** the caraway seeds in a large soup pot over medium heat, and toast for 1 minute. Remove from the pot.

2. **Add** the oil and onion to the pot and sauté until fragrant, about 3 to 4 minutes. Add the cabbage, carrots, beets, potato, and salt and continue to sauté until the vegetables begin to soften, about 10 minutes.

3. **Stir** in the vegetable broth, white beans, and dill and bring it to a boil. Lower the heat and simmer until the beets and potatoes are tender, about 20 minutes. If the soup is thicker than you'd like, add more water or vegetable broth.

4. **Turn** off the heat. Stir in the toasted caraway seeds and pickle juice. Taste, and add salt and pepper, if needed. Use an immersion blender if you like a smooth soup.

5. **Serve** with sliced avocado and chopped dill.

Easy ingredient swaps: Any thin-skinned potatoes for the Yukon Gold / White vinegar or lemon juice for the pickle juice

any VEGGIE FRIED RICE

Any Veggie Fried Rice

Prep to table: 20 minutes I Serves: 4

This fried rice recipe has all the markings of traditional fried rice but without as much oil. What I like best about it is that it's hard to mess up. Once you've cooked it a couple of times you probably won't need to follow the instructions. Use whatever vegetables you may have lurking in your fridge and mix it with cooked rice. It's flexible, but I'd keep the garlic, ginger, and soy sauce. All work closely together to make it delicious.

2 tablespoons olive oil

3 garlic cloves, minced

1-inch piece (1 tablespoon) fresh ginger, grated

2 carrots, chopped into thin rounds

2 to 3 cups chopped crunchy vegetables such as snow peas, broccoli, cauliflower, red pepper, cabbage, or asparagus

½ teaspoon salt

4 cups cooked rice (brown, white, or cauliflower)

3 green onions, thinly sliced

1 cup chopped hearty greens (kale, Swiss chard, or spinach) (optional)

2 tablespoons soy sauce

Serving suggestion: ½ cup toasted chopped nuts (almonds, cashews, or peanuts) / Chopped green onions / Sriracha or garlic chili sauce

1. **Heat** 2 tablespoons of olive oil in a large skillet over medium heat. Stir in the garlic, ginger, carrots, crunchy vegetables, and salt. Sauté until the crunchy vegetables just begin to soften, about 5 minutes.

2. **Add** the cooked rice and stir, pressing the mix down with your spatula to crisp up and brown the bottom of the rice, 3 to 4 minutes.

3. **Add** the green onions and hearty greens, if you want more texture, and stir until the greens wilt, about 1 more minute. Remove from the heat and stir in the soy sauce.

4. **Serve** topped with the toasted nuts, green onions, and sriracha.

BROCCOLI & MUSHROOM STIR FRY with CASHEWS

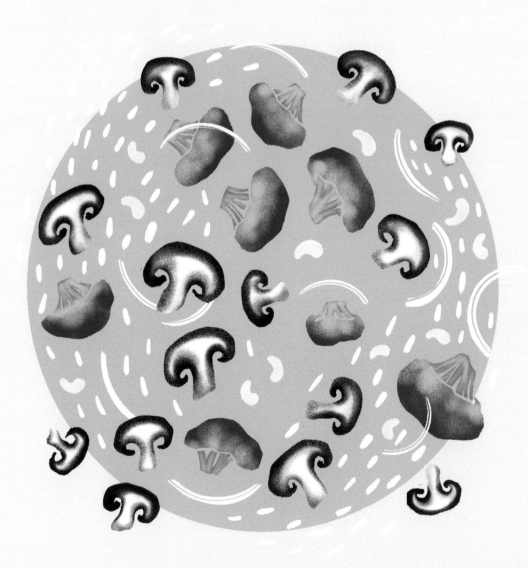

Broccoli and Mushroom Stir Fry with Cashews

Prep to table: 15 minutes | Serves: 3 to 4

In this classic stir fry, cook the broccoli *just* enough to become tender without losing its crisp brightness. I love this dish with cashews but swap in any nuts you're in the mood for. If you want more intensity, trade a red onion for the yellow one and double the amount of red pepper flakes. As with most good stir fries, this one is flexible enough to work with whatever's in your fridge at the moment.

2 tablespoons olive oil

1 medium yellow onion, chopped

½ pound small mushrooms, sliced

½ teaspoon salt, divided, plus more to taste

1 small head broccoli, chopped

3 garlic cloves

¼ teaspoon red pepper flakes

¾-inch piece (2 teaspoons) fresh ginger, grated

1 cup cashews

2 tablespoons rice vinegar

2 tablespoons soy sauce

Freshly ground black pepper

Serving suggestion: Chili paste / 4 cups cooked brown rice or cauliflower rice

1. **Heat** the oil in a large skillet over medium heat for 1 minute. Add the onion and mushrooms, sprinkle with ¼ teaspoon salt, and sauté until the mushrooms soften and the onion becomes fragrant, 3 to 4 minutes.

2. **Add** the broccoli, garlic, red pepper flakes, ginger, and the remaining ¼ teaspoon of salt. Cook, stirring often, until the broccoli becomes tender but remains crisp and green, about 3 minutes. If the veggies start sticking to the pot, add a little water.

3. **Stir** in the cashews, vinegar, and soy sauce, and cook for 1 minute.

4. **Remove** from the heat and sprinkle on a little salt and black pepper, to taste. Serve with some chili paste and rice.

Easy ingredient swaps: Light sesame oil for the olive oil / Red onion for the yellow onion / Broccolini for the broccoli / ¼ teaspoon ground ginger for the fresh ginger / White wine vinegar for the rice vinegar

CABBAGE & CUMIN
STIR FRY with CRISPY TOFU

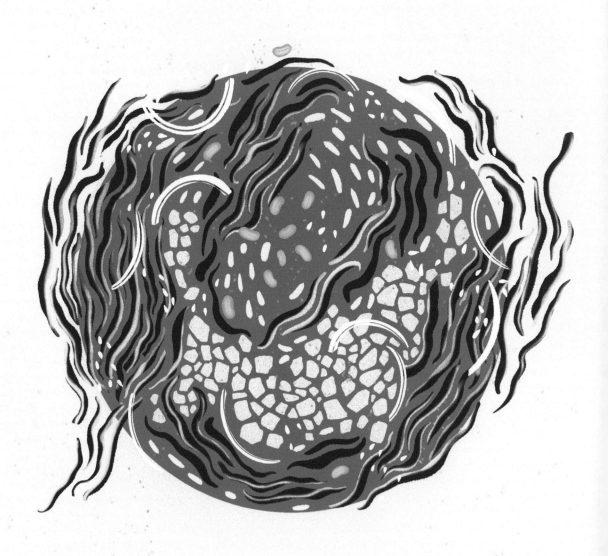

Cabbage and Cumin Stir Fry with Crispy Tofu

Prep to table: 20 minutes I Serves: 4

I like tofu more than most, but if you're not a big fan this recipe could change your mind. It calls on cornstarch, typically used as a thickening agent, to coat tofu and enable it to become the crispiest version of itself. In this dish the tofu becomes a co-star rather than a dutiful addition. The red cabbage adds even more snap and crunch; slice it thin or cut it into pieces. Whatever works for you.

2 tablespoons canola oil, plus enough
    to lightly oil the pan
8-ounces firm or extra-firm tofu
½ teaspoon salt, plus more to taste
2 tablespoons soy sauce, plus more for serving
2 tablespoons cornstarch

1 small-medium red cabbage, sliced,
    roughly chopped
1 small red onion, sliced
1 tablespoon ground cumin
1 teaspoon lemon juice
Freshly ground black pepper

Serving suggestion: 3 to 4 cups cooked rice / Salted peanuts, chopped

1. **Lightly** oil a medium-size skillet. Pat dry the tofu between paper towels so it can more easily soak up flavors. Mix the cornstarch and the salt together in a small bowl. Crumble the tofu and roll it in the cornstarch and salt.

2. **Sauté** the tofu in the skillet over medium heat until it turns golden brown and crisp on all sides, 3 to 5 minutes. Transfer it to a paper towel.

3. **Add** 2 tablespoons oil, chopped cabbage, onion, and soy sauce to the skillet and cook for another 2 minutes.

4. **Add** the crispy tofu, the cumin, and the lemon juice and stir for 1 minute, or until it becomes fragrant. Remove from the heat, taste, and season with salt and pepper, as needed.

5. **Serve** as is, or on a bowl of rice, topped with chopped peanuts. You may want additional soy sauce as well.

Easy ingredient swaps: Olive oil for the canola oil / Rice flour or white flour for the cornstarch / Ground coriander for the cumin / Lime juice for the lemon juice / Walnut pieces for the peanuts

SESAME ASPARAGUS & GREENS stir fry

Sesame Asparagus and Greens Stir Fry

Prep to table: 15 minutes | Serves: 4

This is Chinese take-out elevated by greens — lots of fresh, healthy greens. I include asparagus and snow peas but you can swap in broccoli, broccolini, zucchini, snap peas — whatever crunchy vegetables you feel like eating tonight. As with most stir fries, it's really easy to pull together. Sauté the veggies enough to cook them evenly in the soy sauce and olive oil. Add the toasted sesame oil at the end to give it more nutty flavor. If your sesame seeds are raw, dry toast them in the skillet for a couple of minutes.

2 tablespoons toasted sesame seeds

2 tablespoons olive oil

8 to 10 stalks of asparagus, trimmed, chopped

1 cup snow peas

1 bunch radishes, thinly sliced

3 garlic cloves, minced

½ teaspoon salt

3 cups spinach

1 tablespoon rice wine vinegar

1 cup roasted almonds

2 teaspoons toasted sesame oil

1 tablespoon soy sauce,
　plus extra for serving

Serving suggestion: 3 to 4 cups cooked rice / Sriracha

1. **Heat** a large skillet over low heat and toast the sesame seeds, if needed, until lightly browned, 1 or 2 minutes. Transfer to a paper towel.

2. **Heat** the olive oil in the skillet over medium heat. Add the asparagus, snow peas, radishes, garlic, and salt, and sauté for 4 minutes, or until the asparagus becomes slightly tender.

3. **Add** the spinach and rice wine vinegar and stir until just wilted. Turn off the heat.

4. **Stir** in the roasted almonds, sesame oil, and soy sauce.

5. **Serve** on rice along with sriracha and extra soy sauce.

Easy ingredient swaps: Zucchini or broccolini for the asparagus / Carrots, peeled and sliced, for the radishes / Radish greens, kale or Swiss chard, stemmed and chopped, for the spinach

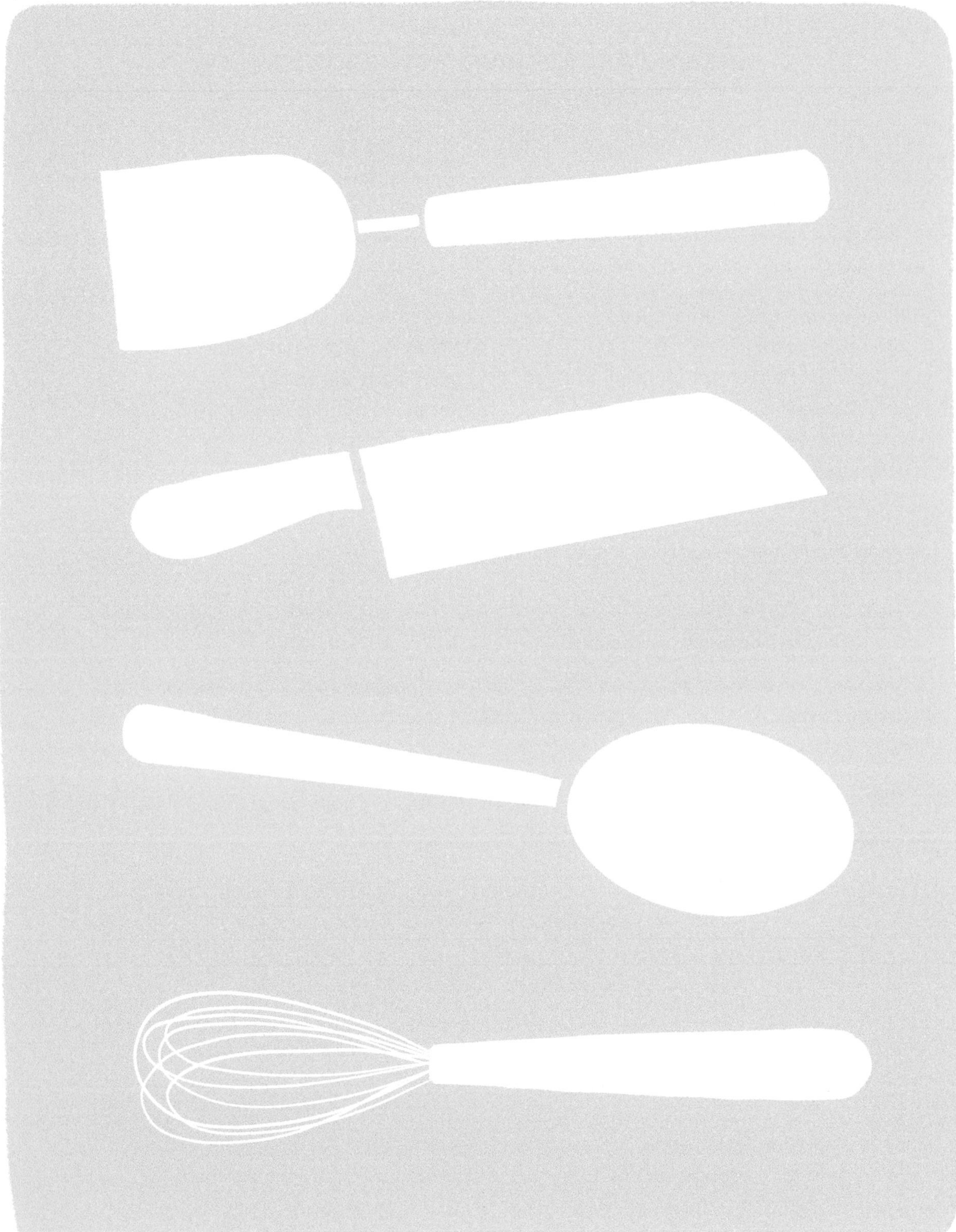

one
RECIPE
three
WAYS

L et's be honest — whipping up a meal every night is not for everyone. Even knowing very few pans are involved is not always enough to make it appealing. So for those nights, when all you want is to open the fridge and withdraw dinner, I give you the following hard-working recipes.

Each starts with one basic recipe, and offers two variations. This means you can prepare the same recipe three different ways — as a grain bowl, pasta, or quiche, for instance. Double or triple the quantities of the basic recipe and you'll have enough to make two or three dinners. It's the equivalent of making a big batch of stew or soup on Sunday to last the week, but more interesting.

As with the one-pots, each of the recipes is a meal in itself — no need for sides unless you want them. Each dish also includes plenty of vegetables, fiber, and protein. But these are not one-pots. The time-saving feature is their flexibility. Finally, each basic recipe comes with serving suggestions, which you can ignore when cooking the other two variations.

If you like this approach to cooking, consider it a starting point for your own inventions. I mean why *not* learn to enjoy one of your favorite recipes served three different ways.

BUTTERNUT SQUASH, MUSHROOM & LEEK *grain bowl*

Prep to table: 40 minutes | Serves: 4

I'm a big fan of butternut squash, which I love for its rich color and high beta carotene content. Pairing it with roasted mushrooms is among my favorite ways to eat it. Add leeks, your mild onion friend, and that's about all it takes to complete this simple dish. Squash and mushrooms are friendly and open to approximately 243 interpretations, so have at it and whip up your bliss. Remember to leave out the *serving suggestion* if you want to rework the basic *Butternut Squash, Mushroom, and Leek* recipe as quiche or soup.

4 cups cubed butternut squash

1 leek, thinly sliced

½ pound mushrooms (any kind), sliced

4 tablespoons olive oil

½ teaspoon salt

½ teaspoon freshly ground black pepper

Serving suggestion: 3 cups cooked brown rice / 1 cup canned or cooked lentils / Salt and freshly ground black pepper / ¼ cup crumbled feta cheese / Toasted pumpkin seeds / Creamy Herb Sauce (p. 146)

1. **Preheat** the oven to 425 degrees. Use your hands to toss the butternut squash, leeks, mushrooms, olive oil, salt, and black pepper on a sheet pan and roast for 18 to 22 minutes, or until the squash is soft.

2. **Mix** the lentils together with the rice in a large bowl. Season with salt and black pepper.

3. **Divide** the lentil-rice mixture into four bowls and top with the *Butternut Squash, Mushroom, and Leek*. Sprinkle on feta cheese and pumpkin seeds, and a little Creamy Herb Sauce, if you'd like.

Easy ingredient swaps: Quinoa for the rice / 1 medium yellow onion, chopped, for the leek / Any salty cheese for the feta / Any toasted nuts for the pumpkin seeds

ONE & DONE: ONE RECIPE, THREE WAYS

Butternut Squash and Mushroom Quiche

Serves: 4 to 6

1 refrigerated pie crust, uncooked
1 cup milk or unsweetened plant-based
   milk (almond, oat, or soy)
3 large eggs
¼ teaspoon salt

¼ teaspoon freshly ground black pepper
Butternut Squash, Mushroom, and Leek
1 cup grated Gruyere, Swiss, or
   cheddar cheese
2 green onions, thinly sliced

How to: Preheat the oven to 425 degrees. Line a pie pan with the pie crust. In a medium bowl, whisk together the milk, eggs, salt, and black pepper. Add the cheese and 1 cup of the *Roasted Butternut Squash, Mushroom, and Leek,* blend until combined. (Save the rest to serve on bowls of cooked grains.) Pour the mix into the pie shell. Sprinkle on the green onions and bake for 15 minutes. Lower the temperature to 350 degrees and bake for another 25 minutes, or until the filling has set. Let sit for 5 minutes before cutting into wedges and serving.

Butternut Squash, Mushroom, and Leek Soup

Serves: 4

2 tablespoons olive oil
1 medium onion, chopped
3 garlic cloves, minced
½ teaspoon salt
¼ teaspoon ground ginger
½ teaspoon ground cumin
¼ teaspoon freshly ground black pepper

Dash cayenne or red pepper flakes
4 cups vegetable broth , plus more
   as needed
Butternut Squash, Mushroom, and Leek
Olive oil
Toasted pumpkin seeds or nuts

How to: Heat the oil in a skillet over medium heat. Add the onion and cook until tender, about 3 to 4 minutes. Stir in the garlic, salt, ginger, cumin, black pepper, and cayenne. Add the broth and bring to a boil. Decrease the heat and simmer to allow the flavors to blend, about 5 minutes. Stir in the *Butternut Squash, Mushroom, and Leek* and heat for about 10 minutes. Serve as is or use an immersion blender to purée it to whatever consistency you'd like. Drizzle on olive oil and top with pumpkin seeds or nuts.

CORN & GREEN BEANS with TOASTED ALMONDS

Prep to table: 15 minutes | Serves: 4

I've loved green beans since childhood when my mom cooked them for me with a little olive oil and dill. Simply add corn, sharp red onions, and garlic and you have the beginnings of a picnic salad — in this case three of them. This recipe is an invitation to capitalize on some of summer's best — fresh-picked green beans and corn. Or use frozen green beans and corn, which have the advantage of coming trimmed, husked, and prepped. I like this dish on a bed of grains, with a little feta cheese on top, served at a dinner table or picnic table. Substitute fresh dill for dried if you are living my fresh herb kitchen garden dream.

2 tablespoons olive oil

1 small red onion, thinly sliced

4 garlic cloves, minced

2 cups frozen green beans

2 cups frozen corn

1 teaspoon dried dill

Salt

Freshly ground black pepper

¾ cup slivered roasted almonds

Serving suggestion: 3 to 4 cups cooked grain (brown rice, quinoa, couscous) / Feta cheese / Simple Salad Dressing (p. 147) or Creamy Herb Sauce (p. 146)

1. **Heat** the olive oil in a large skillet over medium heat. Toss in the chopped red onion and sauté until it begins to soften, about 3 minutes. Add the garlic and cook for 30 more seconds.

2. **Add** the green beans, corn, and dill. Season with salt and continue to sauté until the beans and corn are warmed through, about 3 more minutes.

3. **Stir** in the almonds, and season with salt and black pepper to taste.

4. **Spoon** the *Corn and Green Beans with Toasted Almonds* onto the cooked grain of your choice, sprinkle with feta, and dress with Simple Salad Dressing or Creamy Herb Sauce..

Easy ingredient swaps: Salad greens for the cooked grain

Corn and Green Beans Potato Salad with Toasted Almonds

Serves: 4

1 pound new potatoes
3 to 4 green onions, thinly sliced
Corn and Green Beans with Toasted Almonds
Simple Salad Dressing (p. 147) or Coriander and Lime Dressing (p. 147) or green goddess dressing

Salt
Freshly ground black pepper
Salad greens (optional)

How to: Put the potatoes in a soup pot and add enough cold water to cover them by an inch. Bring to a boil, then lower the heat and simmer until the potatoes pierce easily with a fork, about 6 to 8 minutes. Drain the potatoes, chop into quarters, and toss them into a large bowl. Fold in the green onions and *Corn and Green Beans with Toasted Almonds*, and lightly dress. Taste, and season with salt and black pepper. Serve as is, or on top of salad greens.

Two Bean Salad Dijonnaise

Serves: 4

Corn and Green Beans with Toasted Almonds
1 cup halved cherry tomatoes
1 (15-ounce) can pinto or kidney beans, drained and rinsed

4 cups salad greens
Simple Salad Dressing (p. 147)
Salt
Freshly ground black pepper

How to: Start with the *Corn and Green Beans Almondine* in a large bowl. Add the cherry tomatoes, beans, and salad greens. Toss with Simple Salad Dressing, and season with salt and black pepper, to taste.

garlic-roasted EGGPLANT & OLIVE RAGU

ON POLENTA

Prep to table: 45 minutes | Serves: 4

The original Italian ragu comes from the French term *ragout*, or "well-seasoned meat and vegetables cooked in a thick sauce," according to the Merriam-Webster Dictionary. Standing in here for the meat is smoky, garlicky eggplant and salty olives. When combined with fresh tomatoes and herbs, the dish needs only a bowl of polenta, pasta, or pita toast to complete your dinner.

1 medium eggplant, about 3 cups chopped

½ cup olive oil, divided

1 teaspoon salt, divided

4 garlic cloves, chopped

1 cup halved cherry tomatoes

1 medium red onion, chopped

½ cup pitted and chopped Kalamata olives

1 tablespoon red wine vinegar

½ teaspoon freshly ground black pepper

¼ cup chopped fresh basil plus more for topping

Serving suggestion: 3 to 4 cups cooked couscous or polenta / ½ cup crumbled goat cheese

1. **Preheat** the oven to 400 degrees. Toss the eggplant, ¼ cup of the olive oil, ½ teaspoon salt, and the garlic on a sheet pan, and combine. Roast for 25 to 30 minutes, or until slightly crispy and tender.

2. **Remove** from the oven and mix in the cherry tomatoes, the remaining ¼ cup olive oil, red onion, olives, red wine vinegar, the remaining ½ teaspoon of salt, black pepper, and basil.

3. **Serve** the *Garlic-Roasted Eggplant and Olive Ragu* on a bed of cooked grains and sprinkle with goat cheese and fresh basil.

Easy ingredient swaps: ½ teaspoon dried basil or 1 tablespoon basil pesto for the fresh basil / Couscous for the polenta / Feta cheese for goat cheese

Garlic-Roasted Eggplant and Olive Pasta

Serves: 4

2 to 3 tablespoons capers
8 to 10 ounces fusilli, farfalle, or other
   short pasta
Garlic-Roasted Eggplant and Olive Ragu

Chopped fresh chives or parsley
Grated Parmesan, Romano, or
   Pecorino cheese

How to: Cook the pasta following package instructions. Drain and return pasta to the pot. Mix the capers into the pasta along with the *Garlic Roasted Eggplant and Olive Ragu.* Top with chives or parsley and a sprinkle of cheese.

Pita Stuffed with Eggplant and Olive Ragu

Serves: 4

4 small pita pockets or
   2 large pita pockets, halved
Garlic-Roasted Eggplant and Olive Ragu
2 cups mixed greens

Crumbled feta cheese
Lemon Tahini Sauce (p. 146)
   or other creamy sauce

How to: Halve and toast the pita pockets. Stuff them with *Garlic Roasted Eggplant and Olive Ragu,* mixed greens, and as much feta cheese as you'd like. Finish it off with a sauce, if you'd like some creaminess. Lemon Tahini Sauce, Creamy Herb Sauce (p. 146), or store bought tzatziki do just fine here.

MEXICAN CORN, RED PEPPER AND BEAN BLACK TACOS

Prep to table: 25 minutes I Serves: 4 to 6

On nights I'm unsure of what to cook, I tend to default to Mexican food, the choose-your-own adventure of foods. It's flexible, typically high in protein, and vegetable-friendly. Here, sweet onion, red bell pepper, and corn spiced with a little cumin and chili powder team up to deliver on your Mexican food cravings. Simply sauté these ingredients until your kitchen smells delicious.

2 tablespoons olive oil

1 medium sweet or yellow onion, chopped

6 garlic cloves, chopped

1 red bell pepper, seeded, chopped

1 teaspoon salt

1 teaspoon freshly ground black pepper

1 teaspoon ground cumin

1 teaspoon chili powder

1 (15-ounce) can corn, drained

1 (15-ounce) can black beans, drained and rinsed

Serving options: 6 to 8 (6- to 8-inch) corn tortillas / Salsa / Tortilla chips

1. **Warm** the oil in a large skillet over medium heat. Add the onion, garlic, bell pepper, salt, black pepper, cumin, and chili powder and sauté until the onions and peppers are soft, about 4 minutes.

2. **Mix** in the corn and black beans, and cook until heated through, another 5 to 7 minutes. To heat the tortillas: Put 3 or 4 of them on a plate, cover with a slightly damp paper towel, and microwave for 30 seconds.

3. **Stuff** *Mexican Corn, Red Pepper and Black Bean* into the warm tortillas, top with salsa, and serve with a side of chips.

Easy ingredient swaps: 2 (4-ounce) cans diced green chilies instead of the red bell pepper / 1 to 2 cups frozen corn for the canned

Mexican Corn, Red Pepper and Black Bean Enchiladas

Serves: 4

1 (15-ounce) can enchilada sauce or
  1 (15-ounce) jar salsa
Mexican Corn, Red Pepper and
  Black Bean

6 to 8 (6- to 8-inch) corn tortillas
2 cups shredded cheddar cheese

How-to: Preheat the oven to 375 degrees. In a rectangular or 9-by-13-inch glass baking dish, pour a thin layer of enchilada sauce or salsa and spread evenly. Spoon some of the *Mexican Corn, Red Pepper and Black Bean* into a tortilla, roll it up, and place it in the pan, seam side down. Repeat until finished. Spread the rest of the sauce on top of the tortillas. Sprinkle the cheese over the top. Bake for 25 minutes, or until the edges of the enchiladas are slightly crispy.

Red Pepper and Corn Taco Salad with Lime Juice

Serves: 4

6 to 8 cups salad greens
Mexican Corn, Red Pepper and
  Black Bean
Coriander and Lime Dressing (p. 147)

Salt
Freshly ground black pepper
2 avocados, sliced
2 cups crumbled tortilla chips

How to: Ladle the *Mexican Corn, Red Pepper and Black Bean* over salad greens, and dress with Coriander and Lime Dressing, or a vinaigrette of your choice. Top with fresh ground pepper, a sprinkling of salt, sliced avocados, and tortilla chips.

MUSHROOMS
ASPARAGUS & TOMATOES
with garlic AND COUSCOUS

Prep to table: 40 minutes | Serves: 3 to 4

I came up with the idea for this Mediterranean-style dish after watching a friend toss whole cherry tomatoes onto a sheet pan. Roasting cherry tomatoes concentrates their flavor, which helps explain why I can't get enough of them. Things only improve after adding mushrooms and asparagus. I regularly prepare this simple recipe for friends, usually served over couscous dressed with olive oil and fresh herbs. Double the *Mushrooms, Asparagus, and Tomatoes with Garlic* and make a crustless quiche or pasta dish as well.

3 cups (2-inch pieces) asparagus, with
    woody tips removed
1 cup whole cherry tomatoes
½ pound small mushrooms, sliced
1 large yellow onion, sliced

6 to 8 garlic cloves, chopped
1 teaspoon dried thyme
1 teaspoon salt
3 tablespoons olive oil

Serving suggestion: 10 to 12 basil leaves, chopped, or ½ cup chopped fresh parsley / ½ teaspoon salt / Freshly ground black pepper / 1 tablespoon olive oil / 3 to 4 cups cooked couscous / 1 lemon, cut into wedges

1. **Preheat** the oven to 425 degrees. Mix together with your hands the asparagus, tomatoes, mushrooms, onion, garlic, thyme, salt, and oil on a sheet pan.

2. **Roast** for 30 minutes, or until the vegetables are soft and slightly crispy on the edges. Remove from the oven.

3. **Mix** the basil or parsley, salt, black pepper, and olive oil into the couscous to give it extra flavor and texture.

4. **Serve** the *Roasted Mushrooms, Asparagus and Tomatoes with Garlic* over the herby couscous with lemon wedges, for a nice clean finish.

Easy ingredient swaps: Chopped green beans (trimmed) or zucchini instead of the asparagus / Quinoa or brown rice for the couscous

Lemon-Roasted Mushrooms, Asparagus and Tomato Pasta

Serves: 4

8 to 10 ounces short pasta,
  such as penne
*Roasted Mushrooms, Asparagus
  and Tomatoes with Garlic*
2 tablespoons olive oil
1 tablespoon lemon juice

½ cup grated Parmesan cheese or
  nutritional yeast
Salt
Freshly ground black pepper
¼ to ½ teaspoon red pepper flakes

How to: Cook the pasta in salted water according to the package directions. Drain, and return the pasta to the pot. Add the *Roasted Mushrooms, Asparagus and Tomatoes with Garlic*, olive oil, lemon juice, and Parmesan cheese, and stir until combined. Taste, season with salt and black pepper, and sprinkle on red pepper flakes.

Mushrooms, Asparagus and Tomato Crustless Quiche

Serves: 4 to 6

6 eggs
1 cup whole milk or unsweetened plant-
  based milk (soy, almond, or cashew)
1 teaspoon salt

Freshly ground black pepper
*Roasted Mushrooms, Asparagus and
  Tomatoes with Garlic*
1 cup shredded cheese (your choice)

How to: Preheat the oven to 375 degrees. In a bowl, whisk together the eggs, milk, salt, and black pepper. Transfer 1½ cups of the *Roasted Mushrooms, Asparagus and Tomatoes* into a well-oiled 9-inch pie pan. (You can save any leftovers for a grain bowl.) Pour the egg mixture over the roasted vegetables and fold in the cheese. Bake for 35 minutes, or until the center is set and the edges crispy.

RED HOT *Vegetable* CURRY

Prep to table: 35 minutes | Serves: 4

This dish is a hit with my curry-loving friends. But it works for the curry-shy as well because it can be as intense or as mild as you like. Red curry gives it the heat I like, but swap in yellow curry for something cooler or green curry for a taste that's milder still. Serve it as is, or as the base for Curried Vegetables with Noodles or Red Hot Vegetable Soup. Small tip: Add the broccoli toward the end of the cooking process so it's tender, but hasn't lost its snap or bright color.

3 tablespoons olive oil

3 tablespoons red curry paste

1 large yellow onion, chopped

1 red bell pepper, seeded, chopped

1 medium sweet potato, peeled,
   roughly chopped

½ teaspoon salt, plus more to taste

1 (13.5-ounce) can light coconut milk

½ cup vegetable broth

1 medium head broccoli, chopped

1 tablespoon soy sauce

1½ teaspoon brown sugar

1 tablespoon lemon or lime juice

Freshly ground black pepper

Serving suggestion: 2 to 3 cups cooked rice / 1 or 2 avocados, sliced

1. **Heat** the oil in a large saucepan over medium-high heat for 1 minute. Lower the heat to medium, stir in the curry paste, breaking it up as needed, for 2 or 3 minutes.

2. **Add** the onion, red bell pepper, sweet potato, and salt, and stir until coated with curry paste. Cover the pan partially with a lid and cook, stirring occasionally, until the peppers begin to soften, about 3 to 4 minutes.

3. **Remove** the lid and mix in the coconut milk and vegetable broth. Simmer until the sweet potato is soft, about 5 minutes. Add the broccoli until just cooked, about 2 to 3 minutes. Remove from the heat and stir in the soy sauce, brown sugar, and lime juice. Season with salt and pepper.

4. **Serve** in bowls as is, or with rice. Top with slices of avocado.

Easy ingredient swaps: One medium carrot, thinly sliced, instead of the sweet potato / Two cups packed spinach for the broccoli / Maple syrup for the brown sugar

Curried Vegetables with Noodles

Serves: 4

4 ounces vermicelli rice or bean thread
   (cellophane) noodles
Red Hot Vegetable Curry

¾ cup chopped salted peanuts
2 green onions, thinly sliced

How to: Cook the noodles according to package directions, and drain. Add the
Red Hot Vegetable Curry and heat, stirring until noodles are coated. Serve in bowls
topped with peanuts and green onions.

Red Hot Vegetable Soup

Serves: 4

3 cups vegetable broth
1 cup light coconut milk
Red Hot Vegetable Curry

Two avocados, sliced
2 green onions, thinly sliced

How to: In a soup pot, heat and stir together the vegetable broth, coconut milk,
and *Red Hot Vegetable Curry* until piping hot. Add more broth if you want a thinner
consistency. Serve in large soup bowls topped with avocado and green onions.

ROASTED BROCCOLI
WITH SUNFLOWER SEEDS
grain bowl

Prep to table: 40 minutes | Serves: 4

The inspiration for this dish is the beautiful Green Goddess bowl at Café Gratitude in L.A. I tried to recreate the multi-layered specialty at home but by the 19th step I was over it. All I really wanted was a simple, flavorful grain bowl. So I took the roasted broccoli and added only a few more ingredients, including Cotija, a crumbly, salty Mexican cheese reminiscent of feta. It's just what I wanted. Note: To use the broccoli stalks, in addition to the florets, peel off the tough outsides with a knife or vegetable peeler, and chop them up.

1 large head broccoli, chopped
3 garlic cloves, chopped
1 ½ teaspoons ground cumin
3 tablespoons olive oil, divided

½ teaspoon salt
Red pepper flakes
Freshly ground black pepper
½ cup roasted sunflower seeds

Serving suggestion: 4 cups cooked brown rice / 1 cup chopped fresh cilantro / 2 tablespoons lime juice / 1 tablespoon olive oil / ½ teaspoon salt, plus more if needed / Freshly ground pepper / Crumbled Cotija cheese

1. **Preheat** the oven to 400 degrees. Mix the broccoli, garlic, cumin, olive oil, ½ teaspoon salt, red pepper flakes, and black pepper with your hands on a large sheet pan.

2. **Roast** for 20 to 25 minutes, or until the broccoli is just tender when pierced with a fork. Remove from the oven and stir in roasted sunflower seeds. Set aside the *Roasted Broccoli with Sunflower Seeds*.

3. **Mix** the rice, cilantro, lime juice, olive oil, and ½ teaspoon salt in a large bowl. Season with pepper and more salt, if needed. Divide into four bowls.

4. **Serve** the *Roasted Broccoli with Sunflower Seeds* on the rice bowls, and top with Cotija cheese.

Easy ingredient swaps: Quinoa for the rice / Broccolini for the broccoli / Feta or shaved Parmesan for the Cotija cheese

Southwestern Broccoli, Black Bean and Corn Salad

Serves: 4

1 (15-ounce) can black beans, drained and rinsed
1 cup cooked corn
½ cup thinly sliced red onion
1 avocado, chopped
Roasted Broccoli with Sunflower Seeds

Coriander and Lime Salad dressing (p. 147) or a vinaigrette
¼ cup Cotija cheese or feta cheese
Salt and freshly ground black pepper
Tortilla chips

How to: In a large bowl, stir together the black beans, corn, and red onion. Fold in the avocado and *Roasted Broccoli with Sunflower Seeds*. Add dressing, top with cheese, season with salt and black pepper, and serve with a bowl of crunchy tortilla chips.

Spicy Roasted Broccoli Pasta

Serves: 4 to 6

12 ounces penne, fusilli, or other short pasta
Roasted Broccoli with Sunflower Seeds
½ cup crumbled Cotija cheese or shaved Parmesan

Salt and freshly ground black pepper
1 lemon, cut into wedges

How to: Cook the pasta in a pot of salted water according to package directions. Drain and place in a bowl. Toss the *Roasted Broccoli with Sunflower Seeds* with the cooked pasta. Sprinkle with cheese, season with salt and black pepper to taste, and serve with a few bracing lemon wedges.

Roasted RED PEPPER, ONION & BROCCOLI with PESTO PASTA

Prep to table: 30 minutes | Serves: 4

Pesto is a crowd-pleaser that rarely disappoints. Here, the sauce ties together roasted red onion, crispy broccoli, and red pepper to craft a flavorful base for a pasta, stuffed baked potato, and a wrap. I added chickpeas to build in more heft and protein (and to increase the likelihood of leftovers), but leave them out if you'd prefer. Dairy-free pesto is easy to find in most grocery stores.

1 medium head broccoli, chopped

1 red bell pepper, seeded, chopped

1 medium red onion, sliced

1 (15-ounce) can chickpeas, drained and
  rinsed (optional)

2 tablespoons olive oil

1 teaspoon garlic powder

½ teaspoon salt

¼ teaspoon freshly ground black pepper

½ cup pesto sauce

Serving suggestion: 4 to 5 cups cooked short or long pasta / Grated Parmesan cheese or nutritional yeast / Roasted pine nuts, pistachio nuts, or other roasted nut

1. **Preheat** the oven to 425 degrees. Toss the broccoli, peppers, onion, chickpeas (if using), olive oil, garlic powder, salt, and black pepper on a baking sheet and roast for 20 minutes, or until the vegetables are tender. Cook longer if you want crispier veggies and chickpeas.

2. **Remove** from the oven and stir in the pesto sauce. Serve on the pasta of your choice topped with Parmesan or nutritional yeast, and roasted nuts.

Easy ingredient swaps: Sliced zucchini or chopped broccolini (about 3-inches) for the broccoli / Four garlic cloves, minced, for the garlic powder

Baked Potato Stuffed with Red Pepper and Broccoli Pesto

Serves: 4

4 baked russet potatoes
Olive oil
Salt and freshly ground black pepper
Roasted Red Pepper, Onion, and
  Broccoli with Pesto

Feta cheese
Creamy Herb Sauce (p. 146)

How to: Preheat the oven to 450 degrees. Scrub the potatoes, dry with paper towels or a clean dish towel, and rub them with the olive oil. Poke each potato with a fork at least 3 times. Season with salt and black pepper and place them on your oven rack for about 1 hour, or until soft. Cut the potatoes in half and gently mash the inside of each with a fork. Add a generous scoop of *Roasted Red Pepper, Onion, and Broccoli with Pesto.* Top with a little Creamy Herb Sauce or sprinkling of feta cheese, or both.

Melted Cheese and Broccoli Wrap with Pesto

Serves: 4

Roasted Red Pepper, Onion, and
  Broccoli with Pesto
4 large (10-inch) flour tortillas

6 to 8 slices mozzarella, cheddar,
  or Swiss cheese
Chunky salsa

How to: Lay out the tortillas on the countertop. Spread on a spoonful of *Roasted Red Pepper, Onion, and Broccoli with Pesto.* Top with a slice or two of cheese. Fold in the sides leaving about an inch between them, bring up the bottom and fold over, and roll into a wrap. Coat a skillet with olive oil, heat it over medium-low, and toast the wrap on each side for a few minutes until crisp. Repeat for each remaining wrap. Top with salsa.

SNOW PEA, CABBAGE & fresh GINGER STIR FRY with PEANUT SAUCE

Prep to table: 15 to 20 minutes | Serves: 3 to 4

I created this dish after a busy week at work when I didn't have the energy to do more than microwave a series of Trader Joe's-style dinners. Finally, I couldn't take myself anymore and decided to seek inspiration at the farmer's market. I found it in red cabbage and broccoli and, later, the peanut butter in my pantry. The peanut sauce is divine or — hear me out — simply spoon some peanut butter straight into the pan. With a few minutes of stirring, you'll have warm melty peanut sauce. Insert air high five.

¼ cup creamy peanut butter

2 tablespoons soy sauce

2 tablespoons rice vinegar

¼ teaspoon maple syrup

Pinch of red pepper flakes

1 tablespoon light, or untoasted, sesame oil

4 garlic cloves, chopped

½ head red cabbage, sliced into ½-inch strips

1 small head broccoli, chopped

4 green onions, thinly sliced

1-inch piece (1 tablespoon) fresh ginger, grated

Serving suggestion: 2 cups cooked brown or white rice / ½ to ¾ cup chopped salted peanuts

1. **Whisk** together in a small bowl, the peanut butter, soy sauce, rice vinegar, maple syrup, and red pepper flakes. (Microwave the peanut butter for a few seconds if it's stiff.) Add a spoonful or two of warm water if you want a thinner consistency.

2. **Heat** the sesame oil and garlic in a sauté pan over medium heat and cook until fragrant, less than 1 minute.

3. **Stir** in the cabbage, broccoli, green onions, and ginger. Sauté until the vegetables have softened but still have snap, about 3 to 4 minutes. Pour on the peanut sauce—as much as you want, and store whatever's left over in the fridge. Heat for 1 more minute.

4. **Serve** as is, or over rice, and top with chopped peanuts.

Easy ingredient swap: Lime juice for the rice vinegar / Brown sugar for the maple syrup / ½ teaspoon powdered ginger for fresh ginger / Snap peas for snow peas

ONE & DONE: ONE RECIPE, THREE WAYS

Snow Pea, Cabbage and Fresh Ginger with Rice Noodles

Serves: 4

8 ounces rice noodles
1 tablespoon light or untoasted sesame
 oil (hot or regular flavored)
Snow Pea, Cabbage and Fresh Ginger
 with Peanut Sauce

1 cup chopped salted peanuts
2 to 3 green onions, thinly sliced

How to: Cook the rice noodles according to package directions, and drain. Heat the sesame oil in a skillet over medium heat. Add the cooked noodles and the *Snow Pea, Cabbage and Fresh Ginger with Peanut Sauce* and heat until everything is piping hot, 2 to 3 minutes. Serve topped with chopped peanuts and green onions.

Snow Pea, Cabbage and Fresh Ginger Spring Wraps

Serves: 4 to 5

8 to 10 large rice paper wrappers
 (from the Asian food section of the
 grocery store)

Snow Pea, Cabbage and Fresh Ginger
 Stir Fry with Peanut Sauce
Dipping sauce

How to: Dip 1 rice paper wrapper in a bowl of cold water for a few seconds—no more or it'll get soggy. Place the wrapper flat on a plate and fill with *Snow Pea, Cabbage and Fresh Ginger with Peanut Sauce.* Fold in the sides until about an inch apart, roll up from the bottom, and place on a plate. Repeat with the remaining rice paper wrappers. Serve with bowls of dipping sauce. (I'm a fan of Trader Joe's Gyoza Dipping Sauce.)

SPICY VEGETABLE STIR FRY with TOFU

Prep to Table: 35 minutes | Serves: 4

Stir fry is among my favorite ways to quickly whip up a meal because it can preserve the snap and fresh-ness of a variety of vegetables. This Thai dish makes use of yellow curry, which falls between red and green curry in intensity. Choose your own level of heat, and then consider whether you want to serve this stir fry with rice, in a taco, or as the base of a brothy noodle bowl. It's all good. Use as much or as little tofu as you want. I've recommended one block to minimize food waste.

1 (8-ounce) block firm tofu, cubed

2 tablespoons olive oil, divided

4 teaspoons soy sauce, divided

1 red bell pepper, seeded, thinly sliced

1 leek, thinly sliced

2 cups thinly sliced peeled carrots

1 cup frozen corn

2 cups snap peas, ends trimmed

¼ cup water

2 tablespoons yellow curry paste

Serving suggestion: 3 cups cooked rice / Salted cashews or almonds / Toasted sesame seeds

1. **Cut** the tofu in strips and press it between sheets of paper towels to squeeze out moisture, so it better absorbs flavors. Cube it.

2. **Sauté** 1 tablespoon olive oil, the tofu, and 2 teaspoons of soy sauce in a large skillet over medium heat until the tofu begins to brown, about 10 minutes. Transfer to a bowl and set aside.

3. **Add** the remaining 1 tablespoon of olive oil and 2 teaspoons of soy sauce, the red pepper, leeks, carrots, and corn, and sauté until they're tender but still crisp, about 3 to 4 minutes. Add snap peas and cook for 1 more minute. Remove from the heat.

4. **Return** the tofu to the pan and toss until combined. Turn the heat back on to medium. Stir in the water and curry paste and sauté until well combined, about 1 minute. Add more curry paste and water if you want more sauce.

5. **Serve** with rice and top with roasted nuts and toasted sesame seeds.

Easy ingredient swaps: Tamari instead of the soy sauce / Broccoli or broccolini, chopped, instead of the carrots / Red or green curry paste for the yellow

Cilantro-Lime Curry Tacos

Serves: 4 to 5

6 to 8 (6-inch) corn tortillas
Spicy Vegetable Stir Fry with Tofu
2 limes, cut into wedges

1 cup chopped fresh cilantro
1 avocado, chopped
Salsa

How to: Warm the tortillas by putting 3 or 4 on a dish, covering with a damp paper towel, and microwaving for 30 seconds. Fill the warm tortillas with the *Spicy Vegetable Stir Fry with Tofu*. Serve with lime wedges, cilantro, avocado, and salsa in small bowls for toppings.

Thai Curry Noodle Soup

Serves: 4

6-ounces rice vermicelli or
   bean thread noodles
4 cups vegetable broth

1 (13.5-ounce) can light coconut milk
1 tablespoon soy sauce
Spicy Vegetable Stir Fry with Tofu

How to: Cook the rice noodles according to the package directions in a large pot using the vegetable broth instead of water. Do not drain. Stir in the coconut milk and soy sauce. Add the *Spicy Vegetable Stir Fry with Tofu*, stir until combined, and serve in four large soup bowls. Note: Use regular full-fat coconut milk for a richer soup.

SWEET CORN WITH FRESH GINGER & JALAPEÑO PEPPERS ON QUINOA

Prep to table: 20 minutes | Serves: 4

Looking for new ways to love corn? This spicy recipe gives sautéed corn some nice bite thanks to fresh ginger and hot peppers. Add a cup of halved cherry tomatoes and it also becomes beautiful. Serve the *Sweet Corn with Fresh Ginger and Jalapeño Peppers* on the grain of your choice, mix it into cornmeal and eggs for a batch of spicy corn cakes, or use it to stuff zucchini halves or hollowed-out red bell peppers. The versatility of corn is celebrated here.

2 tablespoons olive oil

½ to 1 jalapeño, minced

1-inch piece (1 tablespoon) fresh ginger, finely chopped

3 garlic cloves, chopped

2 green onions, thinly sliced

1 teaspoon ground turmeric

3 cups frozen sweet corn

1 cup halved cherry tomatoes

Salt

Freshly ground black pepper

Serving suggestion: 2 cups cooked quinoa / 1 green onion, chopped / Roasted slivered almonds / Crumbled feta cheese or goat cheese / Coriander and Lime Dressing (p. 147) / 1 lime cut into wedges

1. **Heat** the oil in a large skillet over medium heat. Add the jalapeño, ginger, garlic, and green onions and cook, stirring constantly, for 1 to 2 minutes. Add the turmeric and cook, stirring, until dark and fragrant, about 30 seconds.

2. **Add** the corn and tomatoes and cook, stirring often, until the corn is lightly browned, about 5 minutes. Taste, and season with salt and black pepper.

3. **Serve** on quinoa, and top with the green onions, a sprinkling of almonds, and cheese. Drizzle with Coriander and Lime Dressing, if you'd like the extra flavor. Offer lime wedges on the side for squeezing.

Easy ingredient swaps: Serrano, fresno, or poblano peppers for the jalapeño / One teaspoon ground ginger instead of the fresh ginger / Roasted corn for the sweet corn / Brown rice for quinoa

Spicy Hot Corn Cakes

Serves: 4

1 cup cornmeal
½ cup all-purpose flour
½ teaspoon salt
2 large eggs
1½ cups plain yogurt, divided
⅓ cup grated Parmesan cheese

Sweet Corn with Fresh Ginger and
  Jalapeño Peppers
2 tablespoons olive oil
Fresh chives, chopped
Salsa

How to: In a large bowl, stir together the cornmeal, flour, and salt. Add the eggs and mix with a fork until combined. Stir in 1 cup of yogurt, Parmesan cheese, and the *Sweet Corn with Fresh Ginger and Jalapeño Peppers*. If the mixture seems too thick, add ¼ cup of unsweetened, unflavored plant-based milk. Heat the oil in a pan over medium heat. When the oil is hot, spoon the batter into the pan, about ¼ cup at a time, and flatten into a circle. Cook until golden brown, 2 to 3 minutes, then flip, and cook for another 2 to 3 minutes. Serve topped with the remaining plain yogurt, fresh chives, and salsa. Your choice (as always).

Sweet Corn and Parmesan-Stuffed Peppers

Serves: 4

4 red bell peppers
2 cups cooked quinoa or rice
Sweet Corn with Fresh Ginger and
  Jalapeño Peppers

1 cup water
½ cup grated or shredded Parmesan
  cheese

How to: Preheat the oven to 400 degrees. Cut off the tops of the bell peppers and remove the seeds. To minimize waste, finely chop the tops of the peppers. In a medium bowl, combine the quinoa or rice with the *Sweet Corn with Fresh Ginger and Jalapeño Peppers* and the chopped pepper tops. Add 1 cup water to a 9 x 13-inch baking dish to steam the peppers. Arrange the peppers in the baking dish, open side up. Fill each pepper with the corn mixture. Sprinkle each pepper with cheese, and drizzle on some olive oil. Cover with foil and bake until peppers are soft, about 35 minutes. Remove foil and bake until the cheese has browned, another 10 or 15 minutes.

SWEET POTATO & RED CABBAGE WITH TOASTED SESAME SEEDS ON RICE

Prep to table: 35 minutes I Serves: 2 to 3

This recipe meets all of my criteria for a simple weekday dinner: It's easy to assemble, nutritious, and flexible — though so are most recipes in this book. Peel the sweet potato or not — I happen to like the extra nutrients you get from the skin so I generally keep it. Include a sauce or not — as noted, almost every recipe in this book is sauce-optional. Use this recipe to create a grain bowl, plate full of tacos, or quesadillas.

1 medium sweet potato, chopped

1 yellow onion, thinly sliced

6 garlic cloves, chopped

½ small red cabbage, sliced thin

2 tablespoons olive oil

¼ teaspoon salt

¼ teaspoon freshly ground black pepper

2 tablespoons toasted sesame seeds

Serving suggestion: 2 to 3 cups cooked brown rice / Lemon Tahini Sauce (p. 146)

1. **Preheat** the oven to 425 degrees. Mix with your hands on a sheet pan the sweet potatoes, onions, garlic, cabbage, olive oil, salt, and black pepper.

2. **Roast** for 15 minutes, before stirring, and roasting for another 10 minutes, or until tender. Remove from the oven and mix in the sesame seeds.

3. **Serve** on bowls of brown rice and dress with a sauce, or just leave it as is.

Easy ingredient swaps: Butternut squash instead of the sweet potato / Creamy Herb Sauce (p. 146) or a creamy dressing of your choice for the Lemon Tahini Sauce

Sweet Potato and Black Bean Tacos

Serves: 4

8 (6-inch) corn tortillas, warmed
1 cup (15-ounce can) black beans,
 drained and rinsed
Sweet Potato and Red Cabbage with
 Toasted Sesame Seeds

1 avocado, sliced
½ cup Cotija cheese, crumbled
Salsa
1 lime, sliced into wedges

How-to: Add the black beans to the *Sweet Potato and Red Cabbage with Toasted Sesame Seeds* in a medium skillet, and heat through. Warm the tortillas in the oven before filling each with the mixture. Top with the avocado, cheese, salsa, and a squirt of lime juice or, if you've got company, serve your toppings in side bowls.

Sweet Potato and Cheese Quesadillas

Serves: 4 to 6

2 teaspoons olive oil
8 (9- or 10-inch) flour or
 whole-wheat tortillas
2 cups shredded cheddar cheese

Sweet Potato and Red Cabbage with
 Toasted Sesame Seeds
Salsa

How to: Coat a large skillet with olive oil and turn the heat to medium-low. Place 1 tortilla on the skillet, add a little cheese and a spoonful of *Sweet Potato and Red Cabbage with Toasted Sesame Seeds.* Add another sprinkle of cheese and top with another tortilla. Toast each side until the cheese is melted, 2 to 3 minutes. Repeat for each quesadilla. Cut each into wedges, and serve with a side of salsa.

TERIYAKI-ROASTED BROCCOLINI & TOFU STIR FRY

Prep to table: 40 minutes | Serves: 4

This homemade teriyaki bowl is healthy, delicious, and almost too easy. All hail teriyaki sauce — the ingredient that makes it all work. Cashews add extra crunch while the dish gets a nice hit of spiciness from fresh ginger. The pro move with tofu is to remove as much moisture as possible so the tofu better absorbs flavors and crisps up. I recommend pressing the sliced tofu between two sheets of paper towels and gently squeezing. Another option is to press-dry the tofu before coating in cornstarch and sautéing. Even tofu skeptics love it.

2 cups chopped broccolini

1 medium yellow onion, cut into ½-inch slices

1 (8-ounce) block firm tofu, cut into
   ¼-inch-thick slices

1-inch piece (1 tablespoon) fresh ginger, grated

2 tablespoons olive oil

½ teaspoon salt

Freshly ground black pepper

½ cup teriyaki sauce, plus more for serving

Serving suggestion: 3 to 4 cups cooked rice / ½ cup roasted cashews / 4 tablespoons toasted sesame seeds / 1 medium cucumber, peeled and thinly sliced / ½ cup chopped parsley or cilantro / Sriracha sauce

1. **Preheat** the oven to 425 degrees. Toss together the broccolini, onion, tofu, ginger, and oil on a sheet pan. Shake on salt and black pepper.

2. **Roast** for 10 to 15 minutes.

3. **Remove** the baking sheet from the oven. Add the teriyaki sauce and flip the ingredients to make sure they're covered with sauce on all sides.

4. **Roast** for 15 more minutes, or until the broccolini and tofu are slightly crispy.

5. **Serve** it as is, or on bowls of rice. Top with roasted cashews, sesame seeds, cucumber, parsley, and a dash of sriracha sauce.

Easy ingredient swaps: Broccoli for the broccolini / One teaspoon ground ginger for the fresh ginger / Light, or untoasted, sesame oil instead of olive oil / Peanuts or walnuts instead of cashews

Teriyaki Roasted Broccolini and Tofu with Rice Noodles

Serves: 4

6 ounces flat rice noodles
Teriyaki Roasted Broccolini and Tofu
¼ cup teriyaki sauce

Sesame seeds
Lime wedges

How to: Cook the rice noodles in a pot of salted water according to the package directions. Drain the noodles and return them to the pot. Stir in the *Teriyaki Roasted Broccolini and Tofu* along with the extra teriyaki sauce and gently warm for 1 minute. Sprinkle with sesame seeds and serve with a few wedges of lime to add a tangy bite.

Teriyaki Roasted Broccolini and Tofu Lettuce Wraps

Serves: 4

1 head butter lettuce, leaves removed
    and washed
3 radishes, sliced
1 carrot, peeled, thinly sliced

3 green onions, thinly sliced
¾ cup salted peanuts
Teriyaki Roasted Broccolini and Tofu
Dipping sauce of your choice

How to: Place the butter lettuce, radishes, carrot, green onions, salted peanuts, and dipping sauce in separate smallish bowls on your table. Serve the *Teriyaki Roasted Broccolini* in a separate dish. Invite fellow diners to take a lettuce leaf, add a spoonful of the *Teriyaki Roasted Broccolini,* and then top with the other ingredients. Fold up the leaves, and dip in the sauce of your choice.

RECIPE-*free* COOKING

Cooking without relying on a recipe, also known as freestyle cooking, can build intuitive cooking skills and make it easy to use up stray vegetables. But without a few basic guidelines, the results can be pretty terrible. Just ask my poor husband who has traveled down some dark paths thanks to my passion for eliminating food waste.

I recommend starting with whatever's hanging around in your fridge or pantry, or maybe follow a craving. There are lots of directions you can take your vegetables, of course. On the following pages, I've outlined how to make them the starting point for a grain bowl because it's an easy way to build a dinner that includes fiber, nutrients, and protein. Grain bowls follow more or less the same set of rules: Start with a grain, sauté or roast 2 to 3 vegetables with olive oil and seasoning, choose a protein, add toppings, and you're done.

To create the starter set of flavor and vegetable combinations I leaned on my own experience and on *The Flavor Bible*, which lists herbs and spices that go well with different vegetables. I highly recommend it if you want to nerd out and explore the vast array of flavor possibilities.

MAKE A BOWL for DINNER

// MAKES ONE BOWL //

step ① - - - - - - - → step ② - - - →

WHILE ROASTING
OR SAUTÉEING

PICK A GRAIN*

one, two, or three

PICK A VEGETABLE

1 CUP (COOKED)

1:1:1 RATIO → 1: ½ CUP

· quinoa

· farro

· white rice

· brown rice

· wild rice

· couscous

* feel free to sub in
CAULIFLOWER RICE, PASTA
or BAKED POTATO

Roast or Sauté WITH
2 TABLESPOONS
OLIVE OIL
(or other fat)

· tomatoes + onions + eggplant

· carrots + potatoes + shallots

· winter squash + mushrooms + garlic

· bell peppers + onion + zucchini

· broccoli + red onions + mushrooms

· radishes + beets + red onions

· corn + bellpeppers + red onions

· spinach + quartered artichokes + onions

· green beans + yellow onions + tomatoes

· potatoes + leeks + cauliflower

· cabbage + mushrooms + potatoes

· asparagus + leeks + snap peas

· sweet potatoes + onions + kale

→ step ③

PICK A PROTEIN

¼ - ¾ CUP

· nutritional yeast

· lentils

· beans

· eggs

· tofu, tempeh,
& edamame

· nuts

· seeds

· peas & split peas

· chickpeas

MANDATORY· ADD SALT!
while roasting
or sautéeing & AFTER
veggies are cooked

**NOTE:
if you're cooking HARD VEGETABLES (beets, potatoes, carrots)
and SOFT VEGETABLES (mushrooms, zucchini, tomatoes)
CUT THE HARD VEGETABLES INTO SMALL PIECES SO THEY COOK MORE QUICKLY

FLAVOR

--→ consider adding -↴

· SPICE COMBOS ·
½ TEASPOON EACH

dill + garlic + onion powder

rosemary + oregano + thyme

basil + thyme + fennel

coriander + cumin + turmeric

chili powder + cumin + oregano

cumin + cinnamon + turmeric

garlic + basil + oregano

onion powder + paprika + oregano

caraway + coriander + garlic

curry powder + ginger + cinnamon

---

step ④ (optional)
PICK A SAUCE

— drizzle on top —

creamy herb yogurt sauce

lemon tahini sauce

simple salad dressing

step ⑤

PICK A TOPPING

— Sprinkle on top —

toasted seeds

toasted nuts

pickled red onions

crumbled feta/goat cheese

grated parmesan cheese

fresh chopped herbs

chopped green onions

avocado

vegan cheese

SAUCES and DRESSINGS

The right sauce can be just what you need to tie together ingredients, lend creamy depth to an otherwise dry dish, and add heat or cool things off. Basically, sauce offers you one more way to bring the love to your cooking.

I share a few of my favorite sauces here, along with a couple of reliable salad dressings. They're all easy to make. Measure and whisk together your ingredients in a small bowl. Or grab a lidded jar (I use old jam jars), add the ingredients, and shake to blend. Pour it on your dish, and store any leftovers in the fridge — ready to zhuzh up another dinner as needed.

Sauces can elevate a dish but few of the recipes in this book actually require one. The sauces are merely suggestions — use them or not. Again, my goal is to err on unfussy cooking. The salad dressings are a little different; an undressed salad is a pretty uninteresting one.

With each sauce and dressing, I've listed a few recipes that pair nicely. Come up with your own pairings once you've had a chance to test them out. Finally, be prepared to trickle in some water or olive oil if you want sauce with a thinner consistency.

SAUCES

Creamy Herb Sauce

1 tablespoon lemon juice

¾ cup plain yogurt

1 teaspoon dried dill

1 large clove garlic, minced

1 tablespoon olive oil

Salt and freshly ground pepper, to taste

Sample recipe pairings: Pita Stuffed with Middle Eastern-Spiced Cauliflower and Black Olives; Spicy Lentils with Rice and Greens; Italian Tomatoes, White Beans and Greens with Farro

Hot Tahini Sauce

3 tablespoons lemon juice

¼ cup tahini paste

1 tablespoon sriracha sauce or chili paste

1 teaspoon maple syrup

Salt and freshly ground pepper, to taste

Sample recipe pairings: Crispy Garlic Potatoes with Mushrooms and Kale; Pita Stuffed with Middle Eastern-Spiced Cauliflower and Black Olives

Lemon Tahini Sauce

3 tablespoons lemon juice

¼ cup tahini paste

2 large cloves garlic, minced

Salt and freshly ground pepper, to taste

Sample recipe pairings: Roasted Cumin Carrots with Fresh Mint and Couscous; Sweet Potato and Red Cabbage with Toasted Sesame Seeds Grain Bowl; Kale Salad with Sunflower Seeds and Lemon Tahini Dressing

Mint Yogurt Sauce

1 tablespoon lemon juice

1 cup plain Greek yogurt

1 large clove garlic, minced

½ cup fresh mint, chopped

Salt and freshly ground pepper, to taste

Sample recipe pairings: Roasted Cumin Carrots with Fresh Mint and Couscous; Balsamic Brussels Sprouts and Figs

Orange and Lime Mojo Sauce

4 tablespoons orange juice

2 tablespoons lime juice

¼ cup fresh parsley, chopped

2 cloves garlic, minced

½ teaspoon cumin

½ teaspoon dried oregano

Salt and freshly ground pepper, to taste

Sample recipe pairings: Cauliflower and Sweet Potato Bowl with Tangy Mojo Sauce; Roasted Broccoli with Sunflower Seeds Grain Bowl

DRESSINGS

Simple Salad Dressing

2 to 3 teaspoons Dijon mustard

½ cup white wine vinegar

½ cup olive oil

Salt and freshly ground pepper, to taste

Sample recipe pairings: Roasted Beet and Radish Salad with Goat Cheese; Salade Lyonnaise without the Bacon; Warm Potato and Baked Cauliflower Salad with Walnuts

Coriander and Lime Dressing

2 tablespoons lime juice

2 tablespoons olive oil

1 teaspoon dried coriander

2 teaspoons ground cumin

2 cloves garlic, minced

Salt and freshly ground pepper, to taste

Sample recipe pairings: Sweet Corn with Fresh Ginger and Jalapeño Peppers; Red Pepper and Corn Taco Salad with Lime Juice; Corn and Green Beans Potato Salad with Almonds

SLICING & DICING

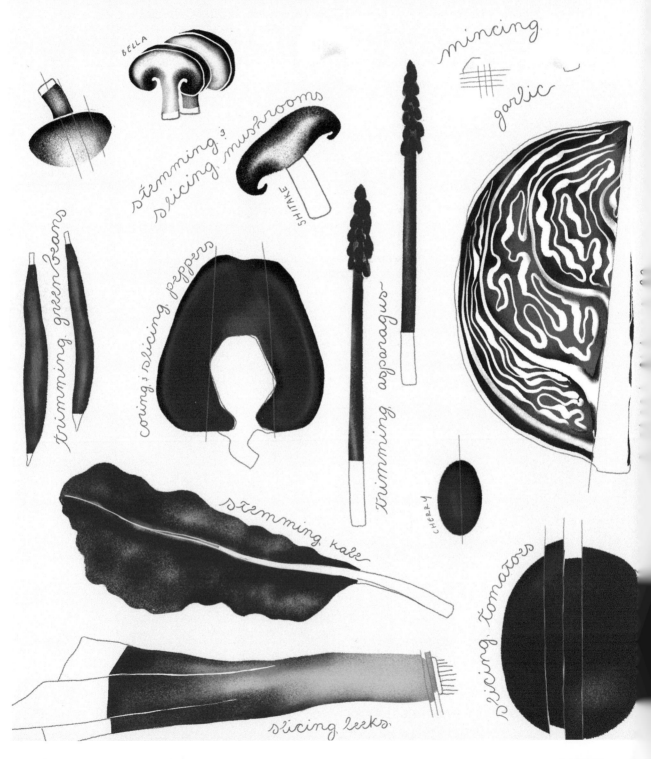

BELLA

stemming & slicing mushrooms

SHITAKE

mincing garlic

trimming green beans

coring & slicing peppers

trimming asparagus

CHERRY

stemming kale

slicing tomatoes

slicing leeks

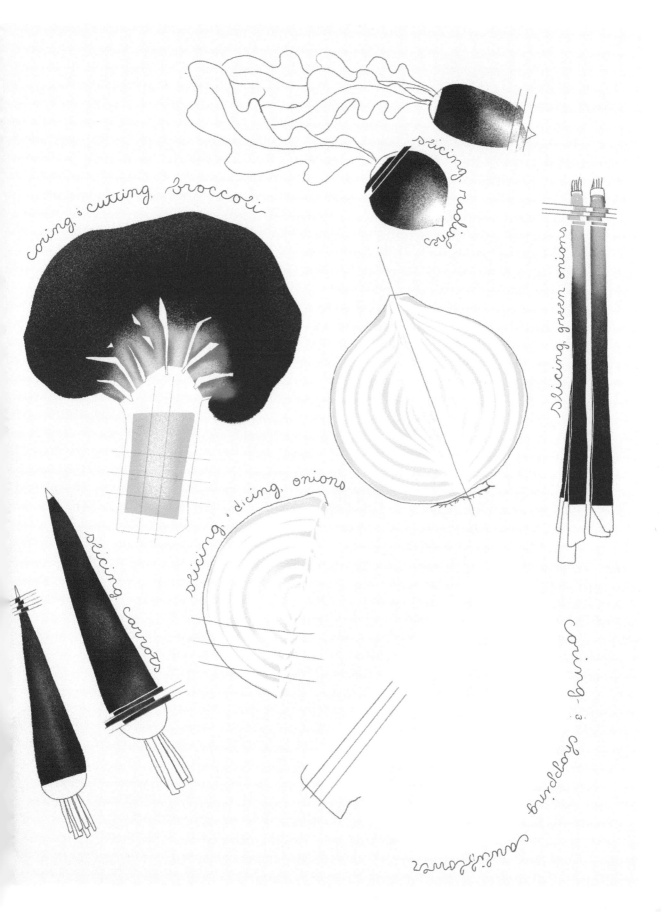

coring, cutting, broccoli

slicing radishes

slicing green onions

slicing, dicing, onions

slicing carrots

coring & chopping cauliflower

Thank you.

To my recipe testing team, for braving many zany Betsy recipes, stirring in genius ideas, and making this cookbook possible. Jennifer Hutzel, Stacie Webb, Toby Webb, Cecile Bodington, Mila Holt, Kip Webb, Amy Treadwell, and Melissa Goleb, you have my eternal gratitude.

To the Stone Pier Press team, one and all, for sharing the *One & Done* story and bringing it to life.

To Amy Treadwell, for bringing your extensive cookbook expertise and copy-editing know-how to this book. Amy, you are a legend.

To Abrah Griggs, for the patience, good humor, and reliably solid guidance you brought to designing and laying out this book.

To every art teacher who tirelessly encouraged this dyslexic girl to keep drawing even though her art was wonky. Thank you for opening my world.

To Josiah, for eating all my testing failures, laughing at my funny and unfunny jokes, and relentlessly encouraging and supporting me through every step of this cookbook and beyond. Love you so.

And to Clare Ellis — words do not suffice. Thank you for believing in me, believing in this book, and charging forward against all odds to bring this book into the world. We did it.

SOURCES OF INSPIRATION

The recipes listed below were "inspired by" or begun with the help of ideas from the following cooks. Thank you, chefs, for sharing your inventive brilliance with home cooks everywhere.

Corn and Green Beans with Toasted Almonds inspired by Kay Chun of *The New York Times* • Red Hot Vegetable Curry inspired by Drew Spangler Faulkner of *The New York Times* • Roasted Butternut Squash, Mushroom and Leek Grain Bowl inspired by Melissa Clark of *The New York Times* • Roasted Red Pepper, Onion and Broccoli with Pesto Pasta inspired by *Eating Well Magazine* • Spicy Vegetable Stir Fry with Tofu inspired by Heidi Swanson of *101 Cookbooks* • Baked Cauliflower with Olives, Cheese and Fennel Seeds inspired by Melissa Clark of *The New York Times* • Portobello Mushroom Parmigiana inspired by Hetty McKinnon • Italian Tomatoes, White Beans and Greens with Farro inspired by Lindsay Mostrom of *Pinch of Yum* • Miso Glazed Cabbage and Walnuts with Polenta inspired by Hannah Reder of *Kitchen Stories* and Melissa Clark of *The New York Times* • Spicy Lentils with Rice and Greens inspired by Melissa Clark of *The New York Times* • Pita Stuffed with Middle Eastern-Spiced Cauliflower and Black Olives inspired by Melissa Clark of *The New York Times* • Braised Mushrooms, Peppers and Tomato Cacciatore inspired by Ali Slagle of *The New York Times* • Cherry Tomato and Olive Pasta with Lemon Zest inspired by Yottam Ottolenghi • Creamy Mushroom and Spinach Pasta inspired by Kirsten Kaminski of *One Green Planet* • Sheet-Pan Gnocchi with Brussels Sprouts inspired by Ali Slagle of *The New York Times* • Kale Salad with Sunflower Seeds and Lemon Tahini Dressing inspired by Heidi Swanson of *101 Cookbooks* • Roasted Beet and Radish Salad with Goat Cheese inspired by Melissa Clark of *The New York Times* • Cauliflower and Sweet Potato Bowl with Tangy Mojo Sauce inspired by Carolyn Casner of *Eating Well Magazine* • Sautéed Beans and Greens with Lemon Zest inspired by Lidey Heuck of *The New York Times* • Swiss Chard and Tomato Shakshuka with Feta inspired by Melissa Clark of *The New York Times* • Fire-Roasted Tomato Tortilla Soup inspired by Alison Roman • Red Beet and White Bean Borscht with Caraway Seeds inspired by *Real Simple Magazine* • Any Veggie Fried Rice inspired by Martha Rose Shulman of *The New York Times* • Cabbage and Cumin Stir Fry With Crispy Tofu inspired by Ali Slagle of *The New York Times* • Sesame Asparagus and Greens Stir Fry inspired by Sarah Copeland of *Edible Living Magazine*

Index

Betsy Freeman grew up in Colorado painting and cooking dinner alongside her mother, who demonstrated how a simple home-cooked meal can nourish body, soul, and community. A professional illustrator, product designer, and dedicated home chef, she lives in San Francisco with her husband Josiah.